THE
GIRL WHO DREW
BUTTERFLIES

THE
GIRL WHO DREW
BUTTERFLIES

How Maria Merian's Art
Changed Science

JOYCE SIDMAN

Clarion Books
An Imprint of HarperCollinsPublishers
Boston   New York

For Jim:

i carry your heart with me

(i carry it in my heart)

Clarion Books is an imprint of HarperCollins Publishers.

The Girl Who Drew Butterflies
Copyright text and photographs © 2018 by Joyce Sidman

Library of Congress Cataloging-in-Publication Data
Names: Sidman, Joyce, author.
Title: The girl who drew butterflies : how Maria Merian's art changed science / written by Joyce Sidman.
Description: Boston ; New York : Houghton Mifflin Harcourt, 2018. | Audience: Ages 10–12. | Audience: Grades 4 to 6. | Includes bibliographical references.
Identifiers: LCCN 2016057731 | Subjects: LCSH: Merian, Maria Sibylla, 1647–1717—Juvenile literature. | Entomologists—Germany—Biography—Juvenile literature. | Entomology—Germany—History—17th century—Juvenile literature. | Scientific illustrators—Biography—Juvenile literature. | Scientific illustration—Germany—History—17th century—Juvenile literature. | Scientists—Germany—Biography—Juvenile literature. | Women naturalists—Germany—Biography—Juvenile literature. | Insects—Metamorphosis—Juvenile literature.
Classification: LCC QL31.M53 S53 2018 | DDC 595.7092 [B]—dc23
LC record available at https://lccn.loc.gov/2016057731

ISBN: 978-0-54-471713-8 hardcover
ISBN: 978-0-35-866793-3 paperback

The text type was set in Adobe Caslon Pro.
The display type was set in Oldbook ITC Std, 1786 GLC Fournier, and 1822 GLC Caslon Pro.

Photo credit for endpapers art not credited elsewhere:
Detail from Maria Sibylla Merian, "Mature Pineapple with Butterflies," c. 1705, hand-colored etching and engraving, P.18,712, courtesy of the Minnich Collection, the Ethel Morrison Van Derlip Fund, 1966, Minneapolis Institute of Art, Minneapolis, Minnesota. Photos © Minneapolis Institute of Art.
Detail from Maria Sibylla Merian, "Rozenkoleurde Akkerwinde," *De Europische insecten,* hand-colored engraving, 1730, courtesy of the Getty Research Institute Digital Collections Open Content Program, Los Angeles, CA.

Manufactured in Italy
RTLO 10 9 8 7 6 5 4 3 2 1

First paperback edition, 2022

CONTENTS

BUTTERFLY GLOSSARY

A compendium of insect words used throughout this book

adult: the final, winged stage of growth in butterflies and moths. At the time Maria lived in Germany, adult butterflies were called "summer birds."

caterpillar: the *larval* stage of a butterfly or moth.

chrysalis: A hard case that protects a moth or butterfly at the *pupa* stage of growth.

cocoon: a covering, often made of their own silk, which moth caterpillars (and some other insects) make around themselves for protection while in the *pupa* stage.

eclose: to emerge from the hard case of the *chrysalis* as an *adult* butterfly or moth.

egg: the small rounded reproductive body produced by an insect or other animal. Maria sometimes also referred to insect eggs as "seeds."

instar: a phase of *caterpillar* growth between two periods of shedding skin, or *molting*.

larva: the immature wormlike form (*caterpillar*) that hatches from the *egg* of a butterfly or moth, grows through several *instars,* and is transformed into a *pupa,* from which the *adult* emerges.

metamorphosis: a series of major changes in form or structure that occur as an insect becomes an *adult.* For butterflies and moths, which undergo complete metamorphosis, the stages are *egg, larva, pupa,* and *adult.* Incomplete metamorphosis (which occurs in many other insects) consists of an *egg,* a *nymph,* and an *adult.*

molting: the shedding of an old, too-small layer of skin.

nymph: scientific name for the immature form of insects that undergo only partial *metamorphosis.* A nymph often looks like a smaller or less-developed version of the *adult.*

parasitism: a relationship in which one organism (the parasite) lives on or within the body of another (the host), gaining nutrients or shelter, and often harming the host in the process.

pupa (plural pupae): scientific name for the stage of development between *larva* and *adult* in insects undergoing full *metamorphosis.* Maria called some kinds of pupae "date pits," because to her, that's what they looked like (also called a *chrysalis*).

The Girl in the Garden

A girl kneels in her garden. It is 1660, and she has just turned thirteen: too old for a proper German girl to be crouching in the dirt, according to her mother. She is searching for something she discovered days ago in the chilly spring air. As she combs the emerald bushes, she looks for other telltale signs—eggs no bigger than pinpricks, or leaf edges scalloped by the jaws of an inching worm.

Ah! She has found it: a crinkled brown cocoon, anchored on a branch like a sailor's hammock. She inspects its crumpled surface: Any change since yesterday? Any sign of the life within? No, not yet.

Her neighbors despise the creatures that fascinate her. They believe that all flying, creeping things are pests, born of filth and decay. If any of them spotted this swaddled cocoon, they would rip it off and crush the "vermin" within, giving no thought to what it might become.

But for years she has gathered flowers for her stepfather's studio, carried them in, and arranged them for his still-life paintings. She has studied the creatures that ride on their petals: the soft green

bodies of caterpillars, the shiny armor of beetles, the delicate wings of moths. She has looked at them closely, sketched and painted them. In learning the skills of an artist, she has learned to look and watch and wonder.

Imagine this girl, forbidden from training as either a scholar or a master artist because she is female. Aware that in nearby villages women have been hanged as witches for something as simple as showing too much interest in "evil vermin."

Yet she is drawn to these small, mysterious lives. She does not believe the local lore: that "summer birds," or butterflies, creep out from under the earth. She thinks there is a connection between butterflies, moths, caterpillars, and the rumpled brown cocoon before her, and she is determined to find it.

This is her story.

EUROPE
1650

NORTH

WEST · EAST

SOUTH

KINGDOM
OF
SWEDEN

KINGDOM
OF
NORWAY

North Sea

TSARDOM
OF
RUSSIA

KINGDOM
OF
SCOTLAND

KINGDOM
OF
DENMARK

Baltic Sea

GRAND DUCHY
OF
LITHUANIA

Dutch Netherlands

Wieuwerd

Amsterdam

KINGDOM
OF
POLAND

THE
GERMAN STATES

KINGDOM
OF
ENGLAND

Atlantic Ocean

Frankfurt

Nuremberg

Bay
of
Biscay

KINGDOM
OF
FRANCE

KINGDOM
OF
BOHEMIA

OTTOMAN
EMPIRE

Adriatic Sea

KINGDOM
OF
ARAGON

KINGDOM
OF
NAPLES

KINGDOM
OF
CASTILE

Mediterranean Sea

AFRICA

Small, silent,
swelling to
roundness,
I do not yet know
what secrets I hold,
what marvels
await me.

A butterfly egg.

Chapter 1: EGG

April 2, 1647 Frankfurt, Germany

Maria Sibylla Merian was born on a bright spring day into a family of printers and engravers. Her father, Matthäus Merian the Elder, ran a thriving Frankfurt publishing shop, staffed by Maria's older half brothers and sisters from an earlier marriage. Maria's mother, Johanna, ran the household.

In a family business in the 1600s, every hand was busy and the workshop hummed with motion. There was ink to be mixed, paint powder to grind, and copper plates to polish and wipe. There were stacks of paper to dampen before printing, and printed proofs to examine.

The Workplace of the Copper Engravers

Engraving by Theodor Galle, after Johannes Stradanus, c. 1670.

Ioan. Stradanus inuent.

SCVLPTVRA IN ÆS.

Sculptor noua arte, bracteata in lamina   Scalpit figuras,

prælis imprimit.

In this scene, a team of skilled workers—like those in Matthäus Merian's workshop—create book illustrations and maps.

1. A master engraver expertly carves his designs onto a polished copper plate using an engraving tool called a burin.

2. Apprentices (craftsmen in training) heat the engraved copper plates on a charcoal brazier, cover them with ink, and then wipe them down so the ink clings to the engraved lines.

3. Another apprentice sketches a map, possibly for transfer onto a plate.

4. A printer's helper places the inked copper plate face-up on the big press with a dampened piece of paper over it. After adding two layers of cushioning felt, he cranks the whole "sandwich" through the press itself, forcing the paper into the thin grooves of the plate and dragging out the ink.

5. The print is taken off the press and hung to dry.

And there were visitors, always visitors. A publishing house attracted new ideas, and a steady stream of explorers, natural philosophers, and free-thinkers flowed through Matthäus Merian's door. In 1647, the world was changing, expanding. The Thirty Years' War, which had pummeled and bankrupted much of Europe, was finally winding down, and intellectual life flourished. Visitors showed up eager to publish stories of their far-flung adventures and strange discoveries in the New World

Natives Extracting Gold from a River, by Theodor de Bry, from *Grand Voyages,* 1591, one of the "New World" images published by Matthäus Merian.

(the little-known Americas). They told of wild "savages" with completely different beliefs and customs; plants with magical powers; and fantastical beasts, bigger and fiercer than any known in Europe.

Lively and chaotic, the printshop was the perfect spot for a curious girl. As Maria watched, her father and his apprentices carved maps and illustrations onto copper plates. They slathered each plate with ink, hoisted it onto a groaning press, and pressed it in to thick, creamy paper. Every

Winged Fish in the Sea, by Theodor de Bry, from *Grand Voyages,* 1594, later published by Matthäus Merian in Frankfurt.

Indians Killing an Alligator in Florida, by Theodor de Bry, from
Grand Voyages, 1591. Matthäus Merian published this well-known
series of volumes.

day, they transformed outlandish discoveries into books. Every day, new
ideas and images flew from the wood-and-iron presses like birds: a river
filled with gold, fish with wings, a lizard as big as an elephant.

What did Maria think of these freshly printed images, hung on
ropes to dry? There were no children's storybooks at the time, and
would not be for another hundred years.
Did these images from foreign lands take
hold in her imagination instead?

Such a small space . . .
I must nibble my way out
slowly, slowly:
greeting the leaf,
greeting the sky.

An egg hatching into a caterpillar.

CHAPTER 2: HATCHING
1650   Frankfurt, Germany

Before Maria could learn much from her talented father, he died while visiting a mineral spring to "take the waters" for his health. This left his young wife, Johanna, and three-year-old Maria in a precarious position. Although a widow would sometimes manage her late husband's affairs, Matthäus's sons from his previous marriage were grown men and quickly took charge of the family business. Johanna no longer fit into the Merian household.

Within a year, Johanna married the artist Jacob Marrel. Marrel specialized in painting ornamental flowers—wildly popular in Europe at the time, especially tulips, which had hundreds of varieties. Many artists like Marrel had turned away from historic or religious subjects. The public was demanding a new kind of art that focused on familiar household objects such as flowers, food, or pottery. This new style of painting was called still life.

Flowers on the Edge of a Table, by Jacob Marrel, 1645. The growing popularity of still-life painting reflected an increased emphasis on the home and personal possessions in Europe at the time.

An engraving from Flemish artist Jacob Hoefnagel's book *Diverse Insects* (1630), which was widely used as a reference for artists. Though beautifully depicted, the insects in this book were not drawn to scale, and Hoefnagel had no sense of their origin.

Maria soon found herself in a household filled with growing things. Roses and peonies bloomed in the garden; tulips and lilies drooped gracefully in studio vases. Their scent, shape, and color became part of her waking hours. So too did the tiny insects that crawled upon them: the beetles and wasps, the bees that floated from blossom to blossom.

Her stepfather prized insects as models and sent Maria outside to capture them. He felt they made his paintings look more alive.

Maria puzzled over those insects. No one could tell her where they had come from. Calves came from cows and birds hatched from eggs,

Geo:4:L:795.   30   M. Vander Gucht Scul:

A woodcut by Wenceslaus Hollar (c. 1654) showing honeybees arising spontaneously from dead oxen. This theory of spontaneous generation had ancient origins and lingered until the early 1700s.

A portrait of Aristotle (384–322 B.C.), a Greek philosopher whose writings on the origins of living things affected Western beliefs for nearly two thousand years. Engraving by André Thevet, 1584.

but insects? Some said they grew from old things—flies grew from old meat, moths from old wool. Some believed that sunshine shrank drops of dew into eggs, which hatched into maggots. Still others felt that fire, as it leapt into the air, produced stinging wasps. When butterflies appeared in spring, people called them "summer birds," assuming they had flown in from elsewhere.

In fact, most people of the time still believed in "spontaneous generation," a theory put forth by the philosopher Aristotle in 330 B.C., almost two thousand years before Maria's time. Aristotle declared that most insects did not come from other insects, but from dew, dung, dead animals, or mud.

At that time in Germany, all crawling things were called "worms" and all flying things "birds." No one connected various phases of insects to one another, and no one knew where to fit them into the natural order. Were insects just early forms of completely different animals? Did butterflies eventually turn into birds, or beetles into frogs? Even scholars of the time believed insects were creatures that God had not fully formed—inferior, even evil in some way. "Every flying creeping thing," according to the Bible, "shall be an abomination. . . . Neither shall ye make yourselves unclean with them, that ye should be defiled."

Mostly, nobody bothered to find out where insects came from. Flies bit and tormented, caterpillars ate valuable crops. They were pests—enemies of man, beasts of the Devil.

But Maria watched and wondered about them.

"From youth on I have been occupied with the investigation of insects." — M.M.

Sheltered
on this underside,
I begin to explore.
All that glittering green
before me . . .
how much of it
will I devour?

The first instar (phase between moltings) of a caterpillar's life.

CHAPTER 3: FIRST INSTAR
1655 Frankfurt, Germany

Art was a joy but also a business that involved the entire household. Along with other chores, Maria's mother taught her how to sew and embroider—important skills in a time when all clothing was made by hand. Her stepfather, Jacob Marrel, put her to work in his studio. Maria arranged flowers and fetched painting supplies for Marrel and his apprentices. Since each studio made its own art materials, Maria learned how to craft delicate brushes from bird feathers and fur, and to grind mineral powders used to color paint.

Marrel also taught Maria how to draw, and she took to it right away. First, she traced the work of other artists: the curve of a petal, the spiral of a snail. Then, using a lightly drawn grid, she duplicated those shapes exactly on a separate piece of paper. Finally, she tried her own drawings freehand, looking closely at the fragrant blooms, recreating their soft petals with washes of watercolor. Following her stepfather's example, she experimented with light and dark, using the contrast to create texture. As a last touch, she slipped in a tiny caterpillar or "summer bird" to help bring her composition to life.

In Maria's time, the best blue paint powder was made from ground lapis lazuli, a semiprecious stone, which produced a beautiful clear blue but was also very expensive.

There are no confirmed sketches from Maria's early years, but this 1669 pen-and-ink drawing is often attributed to her. Note the faint grid lines that would help her copy a master artist's drawing in order to learn proper placement and proportion of objects on the page.

"I was always encouraged to embellish my flower painting with caterpillars, summer birds and such little animals, in the same manner as landscape painters do, to enliven the one through the other." —M.M.

Maria learned how to paint by copying images of her stepfather's. This 1640 painting by Jacob Marrel is from a catalog used by flower merchants to advertise newly cultivated varieties for sale.

Maria grew more and more skillful, helping the studio produce watercolors and prints to sell. Marrel noticed her energy and her deft hands. He knew that as a girl, Maria could not be legally apprenticed, or inherit his business. She could not travel abroad to other artists' workshops to broaden her knowledge. She should not even be encouraged to master oil paints, or paint figures or city scenes. All these, according to customs of the time, were the province of men.

But she was one of the best students he'd ever had. He taught her all he knew of painting flowers for profit.

WOMEN: UNSUNG HEROES OF THE WORKFORCE

Art was big business in seventeenth-century Europe. Artists created beautiful works to enliven wealthy homes, but they were also craftsmen. In the absence of photography (which would not be invented for another two hundred years) artists' workshops provided city maps, illustrations of important events, and detailed catalogs of items for sale. Maria's stepfather, Jacob Marrel, was well known for his beautiful tulip catalogs.

A portrait of fourteen-year-old Sara Marrel, Maria's older stepsister, by the apprentice Johann Graff, 1658. In her lace cap and apron, she is busily stitching embroidery for sale. Maria spent many hours doing similar work.

To control the practice of their trade, craftsmen banded together to form societies called guilds. Every type of craft had its own guild—weaving, baking, ironwork, or architecture. Artists' guilds helped enforce the orderly training of painters, from apprentice (young beginner) to journeyman (young adult who traveled abroad to learn) to master (older expert who ran a studio).

Women were not permitted to join guilds. They were not considered independent workers at all but merely helpmates to their husbands and fathers. Because of beliefs in Germany at the time—that women were physically and intellectually incapable of undertaking responsibilities outside the household realm—women could not formally train in a profession or manage a business. They were banned from profitable crafts such as oil and landscape painting. Their value to society lay in their roles as wife and mother.

However, in reality, women and girls like Maria often learned—and performed—much of the work required of their family businesses in addition to their household duties. They worked just as hard and with equal skill as male craftsmen, and their contributions were essential to their family's financial success. Although not given proper credit, they were the heroes of many a busy workshop.

The world is a plant,
always growing.
I consume it,
leaf by leaf.
The world shrinks,
I grow large.

The second instar of a caterpillar.

CHAPTER 4: SECOND INSTAR

1660   Frankfurt, Germany

Maria loved the work of painting. But the insects called to her too. She lingered outside, hunting for caterpillars. Some were as small as grains of wheat, bristling with tiny hairs. Some were as fat as her finger, pale and hairless. Some sported odd curlicues. Others hung, suspended from a twig, in a tiny, motionless *J* that became a hardened cylinder. Weeks later, the cylinder hung empty. Where was the creature that had snuggled within? What did it look like now? She burned to know more. Were caterpillars, cocoons, and "summer birds" somehow all connected? She had read various theories, but she needed to find out for herself.

There was only one way: she had to rear her own caterpillars and wait patiently to see what they would become. She would observe every change with her own eyes and record everything in sketches and words.

In the spring Maria turned thirteen, Jacob Marrel shut down his studio and left home with his two apprentices for an extended business trip. Freed from her studio work, Maria gathered glass jars and wooden boxes covered with gauze and set up a work space in an unused corner.

She would begin with a silkworm— the one "worm" no one scorned. The silkworm was the only caterpillar of the time whose metamorphosis was well understood. It was considered an almost magical creature, outside the realm of common insects. The strong, shining thread it spun about itself to create a cocoon was highly valued, for it could be unraveled and used

A silkworm (scientific name *Bombyx mori*) perched on a mulberry leaf, its preferred food.

to weave silk fabric (a process first discovered in China around 4000 B.C. and kept secret for thousands of years). On Europe's many silk farms, silkworms were raised for their cocoons, which were unraveled onto spools. Some cocoons were allowed to hatch into white silk moths, which would produce eggs and continue the cycle. Maria had heard stories of this transformation, but she wanted to see it for herself.

It was a perfect place to start. No one would condemn her for studying such a useful creature.

"Because almost everyone is acquainted with the silkworm, and because it is the most useful and noblest of all worms and caterpillars, I have here recorded its transformation." —M.M.

After obtaining a batch of newly hatched silk caterpillars, Maria faithfully fed them lettuce until their preferred food—white mulberry leaves—was in season. They grew amazingly fast—so fast that their skin split open every few days and they wriggled out of it—"just as a person," she noted, "pulls off a shirt over his head." She sketched and wrote furiously, recording all they did.

Science Before Photography

Today, scientists and artists can instantly record and share their findings using digital photography. But in Maria's time, nearly two hundred years before photography was invented, documenting research was much more difficult. A good naturalist needed more than just a scientific mind—she needed artistic skill.

Naturalists could catch, preserve, and study specimens among themselves, of course. But in order to share their findings more widely (in books, for instance), they had to sketch or paint them—or hire someone else to do it. Recording a creature's movements, behavior, or stages of development—as Maria did—meant long hours watching, paints in hand, and the ability to sketch quickly when something happened.

Similarly, there were no online databases to search, or field guides to borrow from public libraries. At the time she began her insect studies, Maria's "database" consisted of bookshops where she might browse any rare works about insects, or studio paintings like her stepfather's that accurately depicted them. Besides these resources, she had only the gardens and fields to find what she needed, and her own paintbrush to record it.

The silkworms were voracious yet finicky. If she fed them the wrong kind of leaves, they died. If the leaves were wilted, spoiled, or wet, they died. If the room grew too hot or too cold or she handled the worms too roughly, they died. Some just died anyway, for no reason she could tell.

"You must take great pains to care for them. . . . If a storm comes and there is lightning, you must cover them; otherwise they will get jaundice or dropsy. They will also die when you give them too much to eat." — M.M.

A silkworm cocoon, the pupa stage of *Bombyx mori*.

She tried again and again, waiting for her boxes and jars to yield the miracle of transformation.

Finally, the biggest, fattest caterpillars began to nod their heads slowly from side to side, covering themselves in a web of silk. Within a few hours, Maria's boxes were dotted with fuzzy cream-colored cocoons.

Now she would wait.

A silk moth after emerging from its cocoon.

Weeks later, busy elsewhere, she may have missed the first few velvet-white moths creeping from their cocoons. She saw them perched on the box's lip, fanning their shaggy, crumpled wings. But in the weeks and months that followed, she witnessed many moths chewing through fuzzy cocoons, crawling out, and pumping up their wings. She witnessed those same moths fluttering, mating, and laying tiny pinpoint eggs of their own. She saw eggs hatch and produce more caterpillars. She captured it all in words and sketches—each chewed leaf, each plump caterpillar, each shed skin, each cocoon. Each soft-winged creature that emerged.

"When the moth wants to come out, it bites through the layers of the cocoon. . . . Its color is normally white and it will take a half a day until it has clearly visible and dry wings, and achieves its moth stage." — M.M.

At the age of thirteen, Maria had watched, waited, and witnessed with her own eyes. And she had created a record of study, just as scholars did at universities.

True, many already knew that silk moths came from "worms." But what about all the other summer birds that fluttered in her garden? What about the other caterpillars she found on leaves and flowers? How many of these creatures were also connected to one another?

If she had studied one transformation, she could study another—even if no one ever saw her work.

Up, up, up
I clamber,
searching for secrets,
full to bursting,
not even noticing
I have outgrown my own skin
again.

A caterpillar's third instar.

CHAPTER 5: THIRD INSTAR
1661 Frankfurt, Germany

Maria continued to collect and sketch caterpillars, making notes as she went along. She was still young enough to roam woods and fields in stolen moments, and to keep caterpillars in boxes and jars.

Soon she would have to give up such pursuits. By age fourteen, she would be considered an adult.

> *"These caterpillars are by nature very timid. When they feel the slightest touch or disturbance, they curl up and stay that way until all danger is past."* — *M.M.*

The future of a young woman in seventeenth-century Germany was rigidly limited. Her first obligation would always be to her household: feeding, clothing, and sheltering her family. She might also work as an artist for a male family member as long as it didn't interfere with her other duties. But traditional academic study was closed to her. No matter how keenly Maria wanted to study "natural philosophy" (the study of nature), women could not attend university, and would not be granted that right for another 250 years. Those in the wealthy classes might hire a tutor *if* their male guardians allowed it, but Maria was not wealthy. She had been born into a family of craftsmen who worked for a living. She was expected to pull her own weight.

And so, in this time between childhood and adulthood, she settled in to learn her trade.

From her mother she learned the business of running the house—how to sew neat, tiny stitches, how to spin rough wool into yarn, how to keep crowded chambers clean and orderly. She learned to choose a piece of meat at the market and season it with herbs from her own garden. She learned household accounting—how to add and subtract bills for soap, candles, and flour. Most important, she learned how to do these things quickly and efficiently, leaving time for the business of the studio, which she much preferred.

The interior of a home in the 1600s. Not many German artists painted domestic scenes at the time; this is from Dutch painter Pieter de Hooch. *Woman Peeling Apples*, 1663.

Shadowing her stepfather and his apprentices, she learned how to select high-quality painting materials, create a pleasing composition, and interest potential customers. The raw pigments used for paints fascinated her: dried buckthorn berries for green, shellfish for purple, precious lapis lazuli for blue. She learned how to grind them into fine powder and mix them with gum Arabic (chunks of sap from the acacia tree), which bound paint to the page. She loved experimenting with differing amounts of pigments and binders, seeking the clearest, most durable colors.

Studio painters, Jacob Marrel included, preferred to paint on parchment (made from animal skin) rather than paper, because it was smoother and less absorbent. The most expensive and sought-after type of parchment was vellum, made from calfskin. While in the studio, Maria learned the finer points of vellum, and it became her lifelong favorite for painting precise, richly colored images.

Ever eager to broaden her artistic skills, Maria visited her half brothers, Caspar and Matthäus the Younger, at the Merian printshop. Breathing in that familiar tang of ink and damp paper, she practiced the time-consuming process of copper engraving, which could transform one design into many prints. Over and over, Maria sank the sharp point of the wood-handled engraving tool, called a burin, into the polished metal, carving up tiny curls of shining copper. She also learned how to etch her plates, adding delicacy to her designs. After coating a copper plate with wax, Maria drew on it using a long, sharp needle. Then she dipped the plate in an acid bath. The wax protected everything but the lines, which were burned—or "etched"—into the copper. It was demanding work that cramped the palm and strained

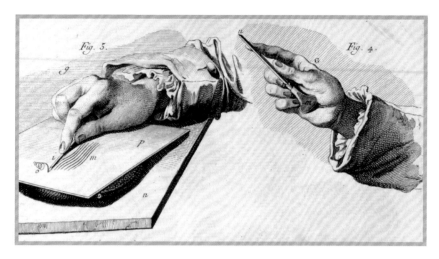

An artist uses a burin (carving tool) to engrave lines into a copper plate. The plate is balanced on a small cushion so that while carving, the artist can hold the burin steady and swivel the plate, allowing for greater control.

the eye. The reward was a design that could be printed and bound into books, allowing one person's discoveries to be seen by all.

Maria also kept her eye out for any books concerning insects. Somehow she got her hands on a newly published book entitled *Metamorphosis Naturalis Insectorum,* by the Dutch artist Johannes Goedart. There, on page after page, were her beloved caterpillars! She pored over Goedart's engravings of specimens he had found in the Dutch countryside. To her delight, he had drawn stages of each species on one page—caterpillar, pupa, and butterfly—which confirmed what she herself had observed. Crucial information was missing, however. Which plants had he found his caterpillars on? And where were the eggs from which the caterpillars hatched? It appeared that Goedart still believed that many caterpillars arose from spontaneous generation.

Goedart was not a university-trained scholar, Maria discovered. He was a flower painter like her stepfather. He had taught himself all he knew

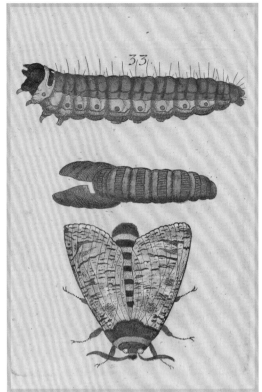

A portrait of Johannes Goedart, and a page from his 1662 book *Metamorphosis Naturalis Insectorum*. Goedart inspired Maria by portraying all stages of a single species of butterfly on the same page. He made no attempt to place his insects in natural settings, however.

about the transformations of insects, just as she had. "I make mention in the following of nothing that I have not observed with my own eyes," he declared. "The only reliable approach to the study of the natural process is through one's own observations." By doing what Maria herself did almost every day—collecting, watching, and documenting—he had added to the world's knowledge of these little-known creatures.

If he could create such a book, why couldn't she?

Because, as her mother reminded her, Maria had grown up. She was now a young woman. And the duty of every young woman was to marry.

I grow quickly,
shedding skin
after skin,
twisting, shifting
to match
my surroundings.

A caterpillar's fourth instar.

CHAPTER 6: FOURTH INSTAR
1665 Frankfurt, Germany

At the age of eighteen, Maria married one of her stepfather's apprentices, the artist Johann Andreas Graff. Johann was ten years older, but he had long been part of the landscape of her life. Her parents made the match with business and stability in mind: Johann gained a skilled, hard-working partner, while Maria gained social and financial security. How did she feel about this decision? Romantic love was considered a kind of temporary insanity at the time, not a basis on which to choose a marriage partner. If she married Johann, she could continue to do the work she loved. Perhaps it was as simple as that.

In 1668, she and her husband had a baby girl, whom Maria named after her mother, Johanna. The couple decided to move to Johann's hometown of Nuremberg, a smaller and more conservative city, where Maria helped Johann establish an engraving and publishing firm. Maria's days were long and busy, filled with housekeeping, child-rearing, and the responsibilities of running the studio.

Nuremberg Marketplace, by Johan Delsenbach, 1730. As part of her housekeeping responsibilities, Maria would have shopped daily in large open-air markets such as this.

She continued to paint, adding to the family's income. Nuremberg's artist guilds, like Frankfurt's, excluded women and prohibited them from selling landscapes, nudes, or oil paintings of any kind (women, considered inferior artists, had to make do with the less durable medium of watercolor). So she concentrated on the decorative arts: flower patterns for embroidery and fabric design. She also became known for her excellent paint powders, which she sold to fellow artists. As her reputation grew, Maria attracted a circle of young women artists eager to learn her skills.

Among her "company of maidens," as she referred to them, Maria experimented with color-fast fabric paints (those that would not wash out) and ever more detailed flower designs. To help her students learn, she engraved a series of elegant flower prints they could use as templates for their own work. These flower prints became so popular that she and her husband decided it might be worth the financial risk to publish them.

The result was Maria's first book: *Neues Blumenbuch* (New book of flowers), published in 1675 (two more volumes came out in 1677 and 1680). It featured the lush tulips, roses, and lilies that had filled her childhood home and were still so popular in European society. In her preface, Maria declared that she offered her designs to all, "to copy and paint, and to sew in the women's rooms, and for use and pleasure of all expert lovers of art."

The book was warmly received. The artist and biographer Joachim von Sandrart even included Maria in his 1675 book *Teutsche Academie*

OPPOSITE: *Turk's Cap Lily,* Maria Sibylla Graff (Merian), from the first volume of *Neues Blumenbuch* (New book of flowers), 1675. Though this was a flower book, Maria included beautifully detailed insects on almost every page.

9

(German Academy of Artists), listing her as "the daughter of the famous engraver M. Merian." She painted, he said, with "great skill, delicacy and intelligence in drawings, watercolors, and engravings," and taught "many others who wished to learn and practice this skill . . . at the same time as managing her household with great efficiency."

She still found time to search out caterpillars, moths, and butterflies, tucking them away in the corner of her kitchen where she could observe and sketch each stage of their lives. As she moved through her days—feeding her family, painting, teaching—she puzzled over what she found. Why did some caterpillars feed on only one plant, while others seemed to eat everything? How exactly did the caterpillars change inside their cocoons? Why did some cocoons produce flies or wasps instead of moths?

She had to be wary in her investigations, though. Nuremberg society, like that of Frankfurt, would frown on a married woman gathering grubs and caterpillars. Only the unclean and wicked would be interested in such pests, they believed.

WITCH HUNTS: THE DANGERS OF BEING DIFFERENT

Nearly 100,000 people—three-quarters of them women—were prosecuted as witches in Europe from 1450 to 1750, many in areas near Maria's town of Nuremberg. Witch hysteria was spurred by overzealous clerics and simple factors such as envy and ill will among neighbors, but the trials were very real. Thousands, believed to be working against God on behalf of the Devil, were put to death by drowning, hanging, or burning. Typical targets were women on the edges of society who exhibited odd behaviors such as talking to animals, wandering the countryside at night, or hoarding insects. They were ostracized (shunned) and often blamed for illnesses, accidents, crop failures, and other disasters.

In fact, at the time, women who followed any sort of intellectual pursuit—especially a study of "noxious animals"—were deemed abnormal. One educator claimed that the mind of a lady was fragile, and "gets entangled in the endless objects to such an extent that [she] loses sight of civilian utility in society."

This engraving from the sixteenth century shows witches being burned alive. From the clouds above, a female serpent representing the Devil gathers up their spirits.

Since her marriage, Maria had followed the path of the lady artist, creating decorative works that sold well. She barely had time for caterpillar collecting, and it did not contribute to the family business. Still, when she held a pupa—or "date pit," as she called it—with its outline of tiny wings beneath the protective shell, she felt the creature stirring within. Somehow, in its silent, dormant stage, this living being was slowly and miraculously turning itself into a butterfly, though she had yet to figure out the exact moment of transformation.

"When put on the warm hand, it started moving vividly and you could clearly see that inside the changing caterpillar, or better, inside its 'date pit,' was life nevertheless. But if cut open too early or after two days, nothing but colored watery material comes flowing out." —M.M.

Others who studied insects were wealthy, learned gentlemen with far more resources than she. But with the exception of Goedart, they used dried, secondhand specimens to form their theories. She had raised these creatures herself. She knew them so well!

Her family depended on her artist's income, yet her passion led her right back to her boxes of caterpillars. Somehow, she had to find the time—and the courage—for both.

The rain comes,
and the blazing sun.
I must find
a safe place
to become who
I was meant to be.

A caterpillar preparing to molt and pupate.

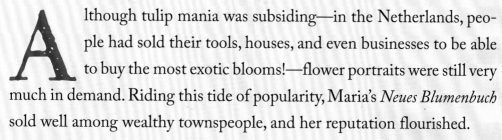

CHAPTER 7: MOLTING
1678 Nuremberg, Germany

Although tulip mania was subsiding—in the Netherlands, people had sold their tools, houses, and even businesses to be able to buy the most exotic blooms!—flower portraits were still very much in demand. Riding this tide of popularity, Maria's *Neues Blumenbuch* sold well among wealthy townspeople, and her reputation flourished.

Maria, however, grew less and less interested in dressing up and accompanying her husband to seek patrons among the rich and influential.

Instead, along with new baby Dorothea and ten-year-old Johanna, she visited the gardens near Nuremberg Castle—gathering, watching, learning. Friends began to bring her specimens to study. Word spread of her insect collections, and interest grew. Curious strangers stopped by to see— and sometimes buy—her trays of pinned butterflies and preserved pupae. Was the tide of public opinion slowly turning away from superstition and toward discovery?

Maria became known as the caterpillar lady. No insect was beyond her scope of interest. One day a neighbor brought her three small birds for dinner. "As I was about to pluck them," she recorded later, "there were seventeen fat maggots ... on them. ... These maggots had no feet and yet they were able to hold quite fast to the feathers. The next day they changed into completely brown [pupae]. On August 26th there came out so many pretty green and blue flies which I had great difficulty in catching, as they were so quick, and only got five of them; all the others escaped."

She was a meticulous researcher. As she gathered live insects, she noted which plants she'd found them on. She kept their boxes clean, bringing in fresh leaves every day. She recorded their behavior and the timing of their transformations. When the caterpillars died or their pupae failed to produce an adult, she repeated her investigations. It was tedious work, but it soon yielded fascinating conclusions.

Maria would have sold pinned specimens such as these painted lady butterflies (*Vanessa cardui*).

Maria now felt certain—based on her own observations—that all European butterflies and moths followed the same cycle of transformation: egg to caterpillar to pupa and back to egg again. Different caterpillars developed on different timetables, however: some became adults within weeks, some pupated the entire winter. And what vastly different pupae! Some shiny, some speckled, some covered in wooly cocoons, some wrinkled and plain except for a curious sling that held them to a branch.

"Sometimes they hang head down from a wall, leaf or stem, shed their skin and within a few hours, as can be clearly seen, look like a swaddled baby. Sometimes they seem to be covered or speckled with gold . . . and sometimes they resemble silver or mother of pearl. . . . Sometimes the caterpillars go and lie on a leaf or something of the kind without spinning a cocoon or hanging themselves up, but first they shed their skin, and then they lie beside it like a veritable date-pit." — M.M.

Mysterious Metamorphosis

Metamorphosis of a Painted Lady Butterfly (Vanessa cardui)

As Maria discovered, all butterflies and moths undergo complete metamorphosis, which means they move through four very different phases: egg, larva, pupa, and adult.

1. Egg

Every butterfly begins as a tiny **egg**, laid by a female butterfly after mating. Eggs usually hatch within a few days. Many newly hatched caterpillars will eat their own eggshells, which supply important nutrients.

4. Adult

When the adult butterfly is fully formed within the pupa, and the outside conditions are just right, the walls become transparent, revealing a glimpse of wings. Soon after, the pupa **ecloses**, or splits open, and the adult crawls out. Its wings are crumpled at first, but the butterfly steadily pumps liquid from its body into its wings. After about an hour, the wings stretch to full size and harden. The **adult** is ready to fly, mate, and (if female) produce eggs of its own.

2. LARVA

A **caterpillar**, or butterfly larva, is an eating machine. For a couple of weeks all it does is munch and grow. As it gets bigger it **molts** several times, splitting the old skin with its head and wriggling out, revealing stretchy skin underneath. In each new phase, called an **instar**, a caterpillar might change color or texture—very confusing to naturalists like Maria. Some caterpillars masquerade as dead leaves, twigs, snakes, even bird droppings, to avoid being eaten.

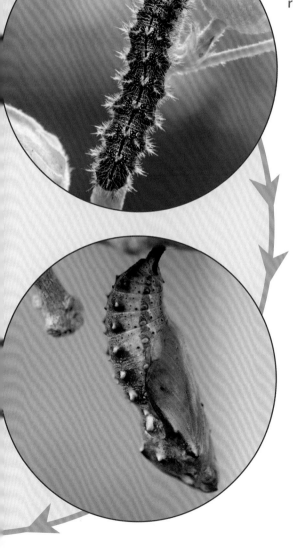

3. PUPA

Once full-size, the caterpillar searches for a safe place to anchor and enter the **pupa** stage. Using a "spinneret" gland just below its mouth, it spins a patch of silk on a branch and grips it with strong rear feet, hanging upside down. Its skin splits one more time, uncovering a tough-skinned pupa, or chrysalis (moths spin a cocoon as well). The pupa hardens into a weather-resistant package that can lie dormant for weeks or months. Inside, the caterpillar's digestive and respiratory systems change drastically. Muscles liquefy and reorganize themselves around groups of cells called "imaginal discs," creating brand-new body parts: wings, legs, antennae, and so on. This process and its timing are so complicated that they are still not fully understood.

Sometimes a caterpillar and its pupa would surprise Maria by hatching into a swarm of flies or wasps instead of the moth or butterfly she expected. Although confused by this, she made note of it, labeling the phenomenon a "false change." Then she patiently collected the same kind of caterpillar again and again until it produced the "summer bird" she expected.

She was also convinced that many butterflies and moths were linked to specific plants. Not only did the adults prefer the nectar from certain

Here, parasitic flies (pupae on left) have killed a saturniid moth pupa (right). Maria did not realize until later in her life that these "false changes"—moth cocoons that produced flies or wasps instead of moths—were caused by insect parasitism. In this case, the fly inserted its eggs inside the moth cocoon. When the fly eggs hatched, its larvae fed on the moth pupa, pupated into flies, and flew away.

kinds of flowers, but they laid eggs only on certain plants. Somehow they knew their newly hatched caterpillars would want to eat these particular leaves—indeed, needed them to survive.

> "These smallest and most humble of little worms . . . are gifted with an intelligence that in certain areas they almost seem to put man to shame in that they diligently hold a timetable whereby they don't come into the world until they know how to find food. So also will the butterflies almost never put their eggs anywhere else, except where they know that there will be nourishment for the young." — M.M.

Brimming with new discoveries, and with Goedart's work in her mind's eye, she planned a new book. This one would include flowers and plants, but its focus would be the *insects* feeding on those plants. Caterpillars, in all their strange and changeable glory, would play the starring role.

Each page of her caterpillar book featured one or two caterpillars, clearly showing every stage of their development. Departing from Goedart's example, she also included eggs, declaring boldly that eggs were the source of every caterpillar despite widespread public belief in spontaneous generation of insects.

> *"I consider it necessary to express much in few words: in general, all caterpillars, as long as the insects have mated beforehand, emerge from their eggs, which have the appearance of millet seeds; and the young caterpillars are at first so small that one can hardly see them."* —M.M.

In another groundbreaking move, Maria perched each insect on its host plant—the one she had found (through much trial and error) that the caterpillar preferred to eat. Maria had decided that insects belonged to plants and plants to insects. Together, they formed a community of living things that nurtured one another. Though her approach was markedly different from the work of others who studied insects, she wanted her book to portray this interconnection—just as she had observed it every day on her walks. Besides, these colorful compositions of insects and plants were much more artistically pleasing than Goedart's rows of specimens on a white background. And she was, at heart, an artist.

In 1679, at the age of thirty-two, she published *Der Raupen wunderbare Verwandelung, und sonderbare Blumen-nahrung* (The wondrous transformation of caterpillars and their particular nourishment from flowers), having engraved every print herself and hand-painted many of them to order. She dedicated her book to "explorers of nature, art-painters, and garden-lovers" and deemed it "a new invention" of a book, in which "the origin, food and development of caterpillars, worms, summer-birds, moths, flies, and other such creatures, including their times and characteristics are diligently studied, briefly described from nature, painted, engraved in copper and published by Maria Sibylla Graff herself, daughter of Matthäus Merian the Elder."

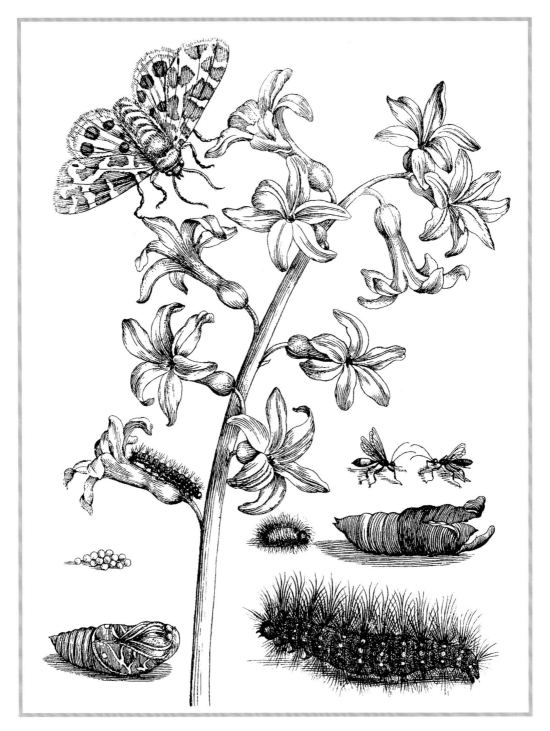

Maria's uncolored engraving of a garden tiger moth (*Arctia caja*) on a hyacinth flower from her 1679 caterpillar book clearly shows all stages of moth development, including eggs. She includes two wasps as well, which were probably parasitic.

The frontispiece for Maria's caterpillar book features the first caterpillar she ever studied: the silkworm, perched on its host plant of mulberry leaves. Her name is inscribed into the branches below.

Her images were beautiful, lifelike, and precise—even scientific in their detail. Her text discussed the metamorphosis of more than fifty moths and butterflies, describing the timing of each phase, her repeated experiments and failures, and any other interesting insect behavior she had observed. She hoped her book would be enjoyed as a work of art, but she also hoped it would help the average person understand—and thus better appreciate—the insect world.

A watercolor study for Plate 23 from Maria's caterpillar book. Maria made sure to include all stages of the emperor moth (*Saturnia pavonia*) on a cherry branch: eggs, caterpillar, cocoon (as well as the pupa from inside the cocoon), and adult moth.

> "Do not, dear reader, let the pleasure of your eyes be spoiled; judge not too quickly, but read me from beginning to end." —*M.M.*

She was the first woman to publish on this subject. Fellow "garden-lovers" and even some distinguished natural philosophers welcomed the work of this "ingenious woman," for many of these metamorphoses had never been observed before. One wrote (revealing the changing attitudes of the time): "It is worthy of astonishment that even women venture to write down carefully what has cost the swarm of scholars such a lot of effort."

I strip
and toughen,
harden myself
into a fixed,
tight bundle.
Then I wait.

A butterfly pupa.

CHAPTER 8: PUPA

1680 Nuremberg, Germany

Encouraged by the response to her caterpillar book, Maria immediately began to gather observations for a second volume.

For her, each day glimmered with possibility. She was entering a rapidly changing but still unnamed field (the word *entomology*, meaning "the study of insects," would not appear for another seventy-five years). Finally leaving behind ancient Aristotelian beliefs, insect scholars had begun to agree with Goedart that direct observation was the only reliable approach to studying natural processes. Such scholars eagerly read one another's work, spurred on by new ideas and innovations. In 1668, Francesco Redi, an Italian physician, experimented with covered and uncovered trays of rotting meat to demonstrate that maggots hatched from the eggs of flies that swarmed the meat and did not spontaneously arise from decaying flesh, as Aristotle had supposed. The Dutchman Antonie van Leeuwenhoek, whose microscopes surpassed all others, began to document insect anatomy in 1673. The Dutch physician Jan Swammerdam dissected countless insect specimens to help dispel the notion that each phase of an insect was a completely different species of animal. In 1669, he declared, "All [European] insects proceed from an egg laid by an insect of the same species."

Scholars like these often had the advantage of a medical education to help them identify what they were seeing. They had the means to devote themselves to their research and the freedom to travel. Because they were men, their work was taken much more seriously than Maria's. She did not pretend to be a scholar, though she read all she could. Nor was she merely an "enthusiast"—one who captured, pinned, and collected insects as trophies. She considered herself a passionate observer who strived to understand the wonders God had created.

But her extraordinary skills set her apart. She had the curiosity of a true scientist, the patience it took to raise insects, and the superb artistic skill necessary to share her observations. In short, she was quietly engaged in some of the finest insect work of her time.

An uncolored engraving from Maria's caterpillar book showing the life cycle of a tussock moth (*Dasychira fascelina*) on a dandelion. Maria deftly combined scientific information with gorgeously stylized leaves and flowers.

"I have had to draw some of them right away, some later when already half changed, and others fully and completely changed; and then draw them again as soon as they had spun a cocoon . . . and then wait to see what would finally become of them. And if anything irregular occurred, I have not let myself become discouraged by the utmost care and effort of illustrating it once more from life; and if false changes occurred in the process, then faithfully depicting those as well." — M.M.

Maria's life would soon change drastically, however. Like a huge stone heaved into a quiet pond came the shattering news that her beloved stepfather and mentor, Jacob Marrel, had died.

Hurrying back to Frankfurt with her daughters, she found her mother distraught and Marrel's business affairs in a shambles. The extended Merian and Marrel clans were fighting bitterly over money.

While Maria settled into Frankfurt to deal with the family crises, her husband remained in Nuremberg. Their marriage had never been close; it was more of a working partnership. But over the years, their relationship had grown more and more strained. Did Johann resent Maria's passion for insects? Did he chafe at the amount of time, space, and effort she devoted to her study? Did he mistreat her? Later in life, she would hint to visitors of her own misery during this period. Or perhaps, in the end, Maria was simply too independent-minded to tolerate the constraints of seventeenth-century marriage.

Whatever the cause of their estrangement, the two rarely saw each other. In Frankfurt, Maria began to focus on what mattered most: her daughters, her mother, and her work.

She published a second volume of caterpillar engravings in 1683. Reconnecting with old friends, she once again gathered a group of female students. But it became harder and harder to balance all the parts of her life. "Everything here is still in great disorder and was thrown into complete confusion during the move," she wrote to Clara Imhoff, a Nuremberg student who remained a friend. "Yet I hope I shall be able to put things in order soon, and then I shall return to work." As her family continued to squabble over money, she grew impatient with the world of human society—so full of suspicion, prejudice, and greed. Her husband visited, insisting she come back to Nuremberg. She put him off. She needed time, space, and quiet seclusion to determine the future course of her life.

She had heard of a religious community in the Netherlands—the Labadists—whose members gave up all material possessions to live simply, away from the whims and fashions of public life. Her half brother Caspar Merian, whom she loved and admired, had made his home there. He invited her to join him.

Abruptly, she decided to go.

In the spring of 1685, Maria put most of her belongings in storage, renounced the world—including her increasingly distant husband—and bumped over rutted roads to the flat, open moors of Friesland in the northern Netherlands. With her two daughters and widowed mother in tow, she escaped to Waltha Castle.

The entrance to Waltha Castle in Wieuwerd, Netherlands, sketched in 1686 by Maria's husband, Johann Andreas Graff, when he came to Waltha to demand his wife back.

Within
a shriveled shroud
I melt, shift,
change.
And from darkness
I wake.
Crumpled and raw,
I crawl my way out
into the light.

A butterfly emerging from its chrysalis.

CHAPTER 9: ECLOSING

1685 *Waltha Castle, Wieuwerd, Netherlands*

Windswept and secluded, Waltha Castle stood on flat lowlands surrounded by a moat and a stately grove of trees. Though connected to the outside world by a series of canals, it was a tiny town unto itself, complete with two windmills for milling flour, a blacksmith's shop, a brewery, extensive vegetable gardens, and a printshop for producing religious pamphlets. Life was communal:

members shared living quarters, meals, and chores. Part of each day was spent in religious meetings, prayer, and study.

Maria and her family blended in as best they could. Renouncing all vanity, they gave up their stylish dresses and wore rough wool robes made by Labadist weavers. They took on a rotating variety of chores such as gardening and soap-making. At seventeen, Johanna was old enough to work and take part in meetings. Seven-year-old Dorothea attended school, which was daily lessons in scripture, Latin, and Hebrew. Maria—relieved to be away from the conventions of society and to reunite with her half brother Caspar—tried to embrace this structured, spiritual way of life.

"I withdrew from all human society and devoted myself to my studies." — M.M.

For a while, she was content. Surprisingly, despite the communal pooling of possessions, Maria had been allowed to keep her paints, brushes, and vellum, which were costly and difficult to replace. Perhaps to prove her skills could be of service, she began painting an illustrated book of useful herbs.

She also finally had time to sort through her jumble of insect notes and paintings from years of flower and caterpillar investigations. Did she wonder if it was all worth keeping? Labadists believed that creating art for pleasure was a vain pursuit. Perhaps, having begun this more modest, contemplative life, she considered destroying the messy pile of sketches.

One of the series of herb watercolors Maria painted for the Waltha community. While portraying dill and fennel plants, Maria managed to slip in a swallowtail caterpillar, which feeds on these plants, as well as its pupa and adult butterfly (*Papilio machaon*).

On the other hand, she had not painted these sketches for pleasure. She had made them in appreciation and wonderment. She believed that all creatures—including butterflies and moths—reflected God's glory and the infinite variety of his creation. Wasn't their astonishing transformation just another part of this marvelous complexity?

"One is full of praise at God's mysterious power and the wonderful attention he pays to such insignificant little creatures. . . . Thus do not seek to praise or honor me for this work, but rather God, glorifying him as the creator of even the smallest and humblest of these worms . . ." —*M.M.*

Perhaps it was her duty to leave a clear, organized record of all she had witnessed, even if she never published another page. And wouldn't it be satisfying—and instructive—to lay it all out in a way that made sense, reflecting those years of work?

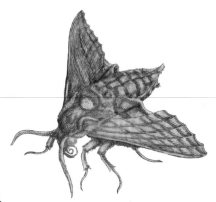

RELIGION IN THE 1600S

In the 1600s, religion permeated life as thoroughly as water or air. Europe was overwhelmingly Christian, and society structured itself around the belief that God's rule over mankind was absolute, as was a king's rule over his realm and a husband's rule over his household. God had created and ordered the splendid, diverse natural world, unchanged from Earth's beginning. (The concept of evolution would not arise for another two hundred years.)

Europe had grown prosperous after the Thirty Years' War, spurring a demand for luxury and worldly acquisition. Communities such as the Labadists (founded by Jean de Labadie, a French cleric) were formed to counteract what they saw as a loss of spirituality in the face of greed. The Labadists in particular embraced simple communal living and sacrifice in order to flush out the poisons of self-love.

Maria had grown up Calvinist, a form of Protestant Christianity with a deep distrust of frivolity and vanity. Perhaps the purity of the Labadist doctrine truly appealed to her. But by moving to Waltha Castle, she was also exercising one of the only freedoms available to women at the time: religious independence. In the 1600s, choosing religious seclusion was a way to flee an intolerable living situation—such as a painful marriage.

Maria obtained a blank master book made of sturdy paper from the Labadist press. Slowly, using her best script, she copied her notes from the past two decades of insect study. On opposite pages, she attached blue paper frames with beeswax and slipped in the corresponding watercolor sketches. Some pages she left blank for future notes and observations. No matter where life took her, this "study book" would be her scientific legacy.

Spring came and Maria grew restless. Her mind kept turning to caterpillars. Exploring the meadows and bogs surrounding the castle, she discovered new insects, species she had never seen. Before long, she was collecting again, adding text and sketches to her study book. She captured both butterflies and moths, studying their differences.

OPPOSITE: Maria made paintings like these in her study book to record her findings as she investigated. She did not sketch in charcoal, but painted her subjects freehand in watercolor with a fine-pointed brush, adding layer after layer of color for depth and detail. Upper right is a stag beetle (*Lucanus servus*) and below it is a plum lappet moth (*Odonestis pruni*) with cocoon and caterpillar. Perched on the leaves are a marbled brown moth and caterpillar (*Ochrostigma velitaria*).

MOTH VS. BUTTERFLY

A male saturniid moth (*Hyalophora cecropia*), showing a fat, furry body and feathery antennae.

Maria called moths "owl birds" because many fly at night, whereas butterflies ("summer birds" or "two-wingers") fly during the day. Moths and butterflies belong to the same order (Lepidoptera) and have similar life cycles, but are slightly different in appearance and behavior:

- All butterflies fly during the day. Most moths, but not all, fly at night.
- Moths, especially males, have featherlike antennae (which they use to sense each other's presence in the dark). Butterfly antennae are stringlike, with knobs at the ends.

A red admiral butterfly (*Vanessa atalanta*), showing a slender body and stringlike antennae.

- Moths have thicker, furrier bodies than butterflies, and their legs are often furry as well. Butterfly bodies and legs are thin and sleek.
- Some moth caterpillars have stinging hairs and must be handled very carefully.
- Moth pupae are usually wrapped in a cocoon of silk threads. Butterfly pupae (called chrysalises) hang from twigs uncovered, but are often textured or colored for camouflage.

Maria also began looking closely at reptiles and amphibians, whose metamorphosis was little understood. She dissected a frog and raised its eggs, recording each stage.

> "After several days, the little black dots began to show signs of life and were actually feeding on the white slime that surrounded them. Following that, they acquired little tails and swam in the water like fish. By mid-May they had eyes, and eight days later two little hind legs sprouted, and in another eight days two front legs. Now they looked like little crocodiles. Later the tail withered and they were proper frogs hopping out onto the land." —M.M.

Always, Maria wanted to know more. Labadist travelers visited Waltha with news of other exotic creatures. Cornelis van Sommelsdijk, the castle's absent lord, had helped establish a Labadist outpost across the ocean in South America: a lush, dangerous place called Surinam. Former colonists staggered back to Waltha after years in the bush, and Maria listened to their tales of tangled jungles and swarming insects. She pored over specimens of huge azure butterflies that van Sommelsdijk had shipped home for his own collection. What sorts of caterpillars had they come from, she wondered? What did those caterpillars eat? And how many more of them hid in distant treetops, waiting to be discovered?

Maria was one of the first naturalists to create a complete, accurate image of a frog's life cycle, including eggs, tadpoles, and adults, helping dispel the common belief that frogs sprang directly from mud ("spontaneous generation").

This pinned blue morpho butterfly from Surinam (a species later named *Morpho menelaus* by Carl Linnaeus in 1758) is part of a collection believed to have belonged to Maria Sibylla Merian.

Then trouble came knocking at Waltha's gates. Maria's husband, Johann Graff, appeared, demanding his wife back. Though legally bound by her husband's wishes under German law, Maria did not want to return to him or to Nuremberg. She argued that because Graff had not embraced Labadist beliefs, her marriage to him was no longer valid in the eyes of God. Labadist elders agreed with her. After a period of difficult months, Graff left. He later divorced her and remarried. Maria resumed her maiden name. She was once again a Merian.

Meanwhile, life in the Labadist community was unraveling. Religious leaders squabbled and left, and money grew tight. When both Maria's brother Caspar and her aged mother died, Maria took a hard look at her life. She had been at Waltha for six years. Her daughters had grown up: Johanna was twenty-three and Dorothea thirteen, which at the time was considered the brink of womanhood. Thanks to Maria's training, they were both accomplished artists and budding naturalists in their own right, but they had been severely limited in other ways. Dorothea's education at Waltha had been confined to lessons from scripture and Labadist religious tracts, punctuated by rebukes and thrashings from the sect's "aunts" and "uncles." And Johanna wished to marry—which Labadist teachings restricted.

Maria turned her sights on Amsterdam, the port city of the Netherlands and the center of science, art, and commerce for all of Europe. Amsterdam was home to fantastic collections of animals and insects from all over the world, and to gardens and hothouses full of exotic plants. Perhaps collectors who had read her two caterpillar books might wish to buy her watercolors—or her carefully preserved caterpillar and butterfly specimens. Perhaps artists were in need of her expertly prepared paint powders.

Could she and her daughters make a living trading, painting, and selling? Might she have a chance both to support her small family and to follow her passion?

She decided to try. Packing up her daughters, her art supplies, and her precious study book, she headed south to Amsterdam.

Slowly
I spread wet wings,
pump, flex,
unfurl
these bright
soft sails
to gather wind.

A butterfly expanding and drying its wings before flight.

CHAPTER 10: EXPANDING

1691 Amsterdam, the Netherlands

After Maria's cloistered life at Waltha, Amsterdam must have felt like the center of the world.

From her doorstep on Vijzelstraat, near one of the city's three great canals, she could smell the tang of salt air, hear merchants hawk their colorful goods, and observe all manner of people thronging the streets. At the wharves, she could watch trade ships from faraway

Maria lived near a canal like this, which was used for transport and commerce.
View of Amsterdam, by Jan van der Heyden, 1670.

ports unload spices, sugar, coffee, silk. Strange specimens peeked from
the stacked crates: preserved lizards and snakes, foreign butterflies, live
crocodiles, even an elephant! Maria could visit libraries full of scholarly
works and seek out fellow insect scholars, collectors, and artists. She could
reconnect with old friends such as her former Nuremberg student Clara
Imhoff (now married), to whom she sent a dish of carmine red paint.

"*I wish in the meantime to perform further service to you . . . for it has been many years since I last heard from all my dear friends, particularly those I had in Nuremberg. I confess that it would make me very happy to hear something from them or see something of them, and although I regard myself as unworthy of it, I would appreciate the kindness of having a few lines to read.*" —*M.M.*

Most important, under the Netherlands' more progressive laws for women, Maria could open her own business, train apprentices, and paint whatever she wanted. In Amsterdam, anything seemed possible.

But there was much work to be done.

Maria and her daughters set up shop, grinding paint powders and displaying cases of carefully preserved butterflies and pupae. If they were to survive, they had to find customers, patrons, and students. Maria sought out wealthy collectors such as Agneta Block, a skilled breeder of rare and tropical plants, who invited Maria to visit her estate. Block's gardens and greenhouses teemed with plants from all over the world. She was renowned for being the first in Europe to coax the West Indian pineapple to flower and grow fruit. Maria marveled at the brown, scaly pineapple with its "tiny sharp hairs." A bond grew between the two women, and Block hired Maria and Johanna to help create a painted record of her botanical collection.

Maria visited other collections too—often called "curiosity cabinets"—such as that of the city's mayor, Nicolaes Witsen. Witsen was a member of the prestigious Royal Society of London, one of Europe's first "scientific" groups. She admired his treasures: corals, insects, seashells, preserved animals, and precious stones. Spectacular butterflies and moths from faraway South America glittered in his cases. Maria often brought her watercolors along to sketch a specimen or two.

A growing pineapple like the one in Agneta Block's greenhouse outside Amsterdam. Block, who befriended Maria, owned superb conservatories and gardens.

CURIOSITY CABINETS: THE FIRST MUSEUMS

Ever since Europeans first set out to discover (and plunder) distant lands, sailors had been bringing back odd and marvelous objects they'd found: shells, minerals, bird eggs, skeletons. Dutch companies dispatched merchant ships daily to all corners of the globe, so Amsterdam was flooded with such objects. Men of means eagerly snapped them up to display to friends. Collecting natural wonders became a mark of wealth, knowledge, and good taste. Some collectors had special wooden cabinets made to display their treasures, while some filled entire rooms. Eventually, the biggest and best collections, often owned by royalty, became what we now know as museums, which were not open to the public until nearly a hundred years later.

There was a whiff of carnival about these "curiosity cabinets." The rarer and more bizarre an object, the more desirable it was. Huge "giant's" bones resided next to jars of pickled "dragon" embryos. But collections also provided more serious scholars with specimens that helped them formulate theories on the natural order of life. Maria herself credited some of Amsterdam's famous insect collectors for aiding her investigations. And almost 150 years later, Charles Darwin used his own extensive collections from his voyage aboard the HMS *Beagle* to verify his ideas about evolution.

OPPOSITE: An image of one of the "curiosity cabinets" Maria visited in Amsterdam, belonging to the Dutch East Indies merchant Livinus Vincent.

TAB. VII.

Pinac. 11.

Pinac. 12.

N° 15.

Maria was now a working artist: buying, selling, and painting for others. Any creatures she gathered she quickly prepared for sale. In another letter to Clara, she matter-of-factly outlined the best way to preserve specimens: "Snakes and similar animals are put in jars filled with ordinary brandy, and the jars are well sealed with wood . . . and if one wishes to kill butterflies quickly, then one must hold the point of a darning needle in a flame until hot or glowing red, and stick it into the butterfly. They die immediately with no damage to their wings."

Her hard work soon paid off. Within a few years, she was able to move to a larger house with her younger daughter, Dorothea. Johanna had married Jacob Henrik Herolt, a merchant and former Labadist with trading connections in Surinam. Using skills gleaned from her mother, Johanna was able to launch her own artistic career in Amsterdam.

In this bustling, modern city, Maria now lived independently as an artist and businesswoman. Scholars, physicians, and botanists sought her out to share new discoveries. It was a busy, active life, but with little room for her first love: observation and discovery. In spare moments, she still tried to gather caterpillars and record their metamorphoses, continually fascinated by new forms of this cyclical pattern. But as a single woman supporting her daughter, she had little time for such exploration. Entries in her study book dwindled and then stopped altogether.

Peering into cases of exotic butterflies from distant lands—glittering even in death—Maria once again felt a deep longing to know more about them. How did these magnificent creatures live? What plants did they eat? How did they grow and change?

She doubted what some said, that in the tropics, toads magically appeared when water was tossed on the ground. Or that plants spontaneously transformed into caterpillars, or moths into birds, simply because the climate was so hot and wild.

In Amsterdam, Maria would have seen butterfly collections such as this one, showing specimens from all over the world.

She suspected that tropical creatures followed the same pattern of transformation she had discovered in so many European species. Though she hunted through scores of insect collections and handled innumerable specimens, no one could give her the answers she sought. No one knew enough to connect butterflies with their pupae, and neither had they recorded what various caterpillar specimens ate or how they behaved as they grew.

"In these collections, I saw countless other insects, but in a manner that lacked both their place of origin and how they reproduced, that is to say how they changed from caterpillars to chrysalises and so on." —*M.M.*

As before, if she wanted to know for certain, she would have to find out for herself.

The idea of a voyage to Surinam began to take hold. This South American country was rumored to be wild and inhospitable, but she had contacts in the Dutch colony there, through her son-in-law and other former Labadists.

OPPOSITE: Map of the world, circa 1700, showing Maria's voyage.

Could she do it? Could she finance the trip by herself? No one had ever traveled to the New World on a purely scientific mission. Certainly no *woman* had made the trip alone, unaccompanied by a male companion or sponsor. Could she travel halfway around the world, braving the very real dangers of pirates, shipwreck, and disease, to face a wild and unknown land?

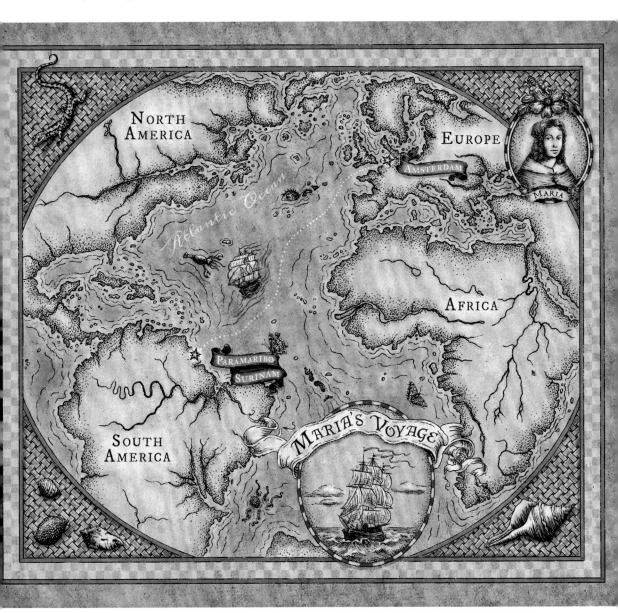

How vast
the swirling dome
of the sky!
How strong the wings
I have grown
for myself!

A butterfly in flight.

Chapter II: FLIGHT

1699 Paramaribo, Surinam, South America

In late summer, after two months at sea, Maria and her younger daughter, twenty-one-year-old Dorothea, glided toward the low green shores of Surinam on the northern coast of South America. Behind them glittered the astounding ocean with its heaving storms, flying fish, breaching whales, and curls of phosphorescent waves. Behind them too were months of planning, making a will, selling over 250 paintings to raise funds, buying supplies, and overcoming countless obstacles to this extraordinary journey of two unaccompanied females, bound on their own scientific venture.

It could not have been an easy trip. Inside the three-masted sailing ship, their berths were tiny and cluttered with luggage and supplies. Meals were meager and repetitive: salt pork, stale biscuits, and whatever fish could be caught by the crew. Every storm must have reminded them of countless stories of shipwrecks and disaster. None of this stopped Maria from continuing her experiments, however. She wrote in her study book of feeding aspen leaves to a box of dark-headed caterpillars she'd brought along.

Map of Surinam in 1700.

Now, before them, brilliant flocks of wading birds picked their way among tangled mangroves. Between tidal mudflats, a thick plume of silt flowed from the Surinam River, guiding them upstream to the frontier town of Paramaribo.

Surinam, also known as Dutch Guyana, was both beautiful and disturbing to Maria. The air shimmered with flowers, birds, and insects, but the dense heat suffocated. The white wooden houses of Paramaribo stood in orderly Dutch fashion along streets paved with crushed seashells. But the docks echoed with the cries of enslaved Africans bought, sold, and branded in the burning sun. Maria soon learned that this colony in Surinam existed for a single purpose only: to grow and harvest sugar. Sugarcane plantations stretched in all directions, worked by imported slaves and native Arawak Indians who were pressed into service by Dutch and Portuguese plantation owners. It was impossible to escape the ruthless business of sugarcane as slaves cut, pounded, boiled, and poured it into sticky barrels, bound for Europe.

Maria avoided the sugar trade as much as possible. She rented a house, cultivated a large garden, and plunged into the work of discovering and breeding caterpillars.

OPPOSITE: *Plantation in Surinam,* by Dirk Valkenburg, 1707. Several Amerindians appear in the foreground, while the plantation owner's residence can be seen along the horizon.

Stuart 1787

SLAVERY IN SURINAM

Enslaved Africans working to produce sugar on a West Indies
plantation, based on an image by Theodore de Bry, 1590.

The history of slavery in the Dutch colony of Surinam was a long and brutal one. To work their sugar fields, Dutch and Portuguese plantation owners had first tried to enslave the native Amerindians, but unrest and escape attempts grew so high that the practice was finally outlawed. Desiring cheap, expendable labor, colonists imported nearly eight thousand Africans from the western and southern parts of the continent in the mid-1600s. In this grim but lucrative "Trade Triangle," Dutch ships (among others) sailed from the Netherlands to the western coast of Africa, full of goods such as cloth, rum, and guns, which they bartered for gold and slaves. Enslaved Africans crossed the stormy Atlantic chained together and packed into airless cargo-holds in groups of four to five hundred. Many did not survive the voyage. Once the ship arrived in Surinam, the slaves were sold at auction to plantation owners. The "slavers" then loaded their ships with barrels of sugar and sailed back to Europe to begin the cruel process all over again.

Work on sugar plantations was backbreaking, and treatment inhumane. Many Africans died of malnutrition, overwork, or injuries inflicted by punishments—and were merely replaced by a fresh crop from the slave boats. Escaped slaves called "maroons" led revolt after revolt until slavery was finally abolished in Surinam in 1863.

Maria quickly adopted the local Arawak-Dutch dialect, asking her native servants for information about both insects and plants. She listened carefully, transcribing what they said. Soon both native and African women were bringing her specimens and describing uses for each leaf, worm, and beetle. What she learned of these women's lives fascinated but also shocked and appalled her.

> *"The Indians, who are not treated well in the service of the Dutch, use [this seed] to abort their children, in order that their children will not become slaves like them. The black women slaves from Guinea and Angola . . . will sometimes kill themselves because of the harsh treatment that is meted out to them, for they are convinced that if they do so, they will be born free again in their native country. This they have told me from their own mouths."* — M.M.

As a white European woman of her time, Maria may have viewed slavery as part of colony life. She may even have borrowed slaves while in Surinam; she mentions both "servants" and "slaves" that helped her plant, gather specimens, and travel through the jungle. Unlike most colonists, however, who believed that the Africans and Amerindians were "rough, wild people, naked, with no God or religious service," Maria embraced their customs and lore. She tasted their food, observed their rituals, and admired their clothing. Of the Surinamese cotton plant, she wrote, "The Indians put its green leaves on wounds in order to cool and heal them." And of the cashew apple: "Whenever it is grilled, it is good against diarrhea and gets rid of worms and tastes like chestnuts." She noted that native girls "string [musk seeds] on a silk thread and tie them around their arms to adorn themselves," and that with a certain red powder from the Rocu tree "the Indians draw all kinds of figures on their naked skin which is their form of decoration."

Still, Maria's main purpose in Surinam was recording insects, and the sheer number of them was staggering. Everywhere she looked, extraordinary creatures hatched, grew, and changed. They dropped from trees, wriggled from cocoons, buzzed around her as she painted. Some caterpillars were huge and smooth-skinned. Some had delicate, branching antlers. Some changed color every time they molted. Some scampered about and hung on to one another; some were sluggish and did nothing but eat.

The butterflies, tilting and sailing over glossy fruit trees, were like nothing she had ever seen. Some were bigger than her hand, some faster than birds! Using her magnifying glass, she peered at their wings and discovered a series of scales overlapping in regular patterns, "like the feathers of multicolored chickens."

ABOVE AND OPPOSITE: Maria delighted in the diversity of insects in Surinam and carefully painted them all, from stinging caterpillars (left) to tarantulas (right). Insects on these pages were later identified by scientists as follows:

1. Scalloped owl butterfly (*Opsiphanes quiteria*)
2. Sphinx moth with pupa and green caterpillar (*Manduca sexta*)
3. Painted jezebel (*Delias hyparete*)
4. Skipper (*Hesperiidae*)
5. Stinging flannel moth caterpillar (*Megalopygidae*)
6. Treehopper (*Membracidae*)
7. Pinktoe tarantula (*Avicularia avicularia*)
8. Two praying mantids (*Stagmatoptera*)
9. Two long-horned beetles (*Cerambycidae*)

Close-up of a blue morpho butterfly (*Morpho menelaus*).

"One day I wandered far out into the wilderness . . . I took this caterpillar home with me and it rapidly changed into a pale wood-colored chrysalis, like the one here lying on the twig; two weeks later . . . this most beautiful butterfly emerged, looking like polished silver overlaid with the loveliest ultramarine green and purple, and indescribably beautiful; its beauty cannot possibly be rendered with the paintbrush." — M.M.

The plants were almost as fascinating. Pineapples, which she had first seen in Agneta Block's greenhouse, grew everywhere in Surinam and tasted heavenly, "as if one had mixed together grapes, apricots, red currants, apples and pears.... When one cuts into it, the whole room smells of them." Thick-skinned banana clumps, pungent sprays of jasmine, black-seeded papayas, and delicate pods of vanilla all astonished her. None of her fellow colonists could tell her anything about these plants. They cared for nothing but the profits of sugarcane.

Maria loved tasting (and painting) all kinds of new fruits she found in Surinam, such as this papaya.

> *"People there do not have a desire to investigate. . . . Indeed, they ridiculed me for looking at anything else in the country except sugar."* — *M.M.*

Life was secluded but never dull. One night, asleep in the dense tropical dark, Maria and Dorothea heard a loud clatter and buzzing somewhere in the house. Lighting a candle, they traced the noise to one of their collection boxes: "We opened [a box] with astonishment, but then, with even greater astonishment we threw it down on the floor as there was a flame of light when we opened the box. Out of it came a number of creatures [most likely lantern flies] and a number of flames. We quieted ourselves down and gathered up the creatures again and were very astonished at their brightness."

Even with her strong, brave, well-trained daughter at her side, Maria struggled in this land of eternal summer. The sticky heat weighed on her. She and Dorothea could barely keep up with all the various stages of their ongoing experiments. The careful methods they'd used in Europe did not work well here. They collected so many caterpillars that it was difficult to keep track of all their food sources. If a caterpillar died before pupating, there was no guarantee they would be able to find that particular species again—or its host plant—in the riot of vegetation. Many caterpillars looked almost identical to one another but ate different foods and hatched into very different adults. And there was always the danger that a voracious army of ants would swarm through, eating up their specimens and leaving trees and bushes "clean as the handle of a broom." Would she be able to organize, sketch, and gather enough specimens to recoup all the hard-earned money spent on this voyage?

Maria was intrigued with both the noisy cicada (*Fidicina mannifera*)—the green insect at center left with wings—and the spectacular peanut-headed lantern fly (*Fulgora laternaria*)—three shown here. Despite its name and its shiny shell, the lantern fly does not actually glow, so Maria's mention of a "flame of light" was probably the result of reflected candlelight. She never found the nymph stage of the lantern fly. The nymph here, perched on an open flower, is an inaccurate combination of these two insects, which locals assured her were related.

In this painting, Maria includes the multitude of ants and spiders she encountered in Surinam, including leaf-cutter ants, which formed "living bridges" by grasping on to one another, and tarantula spiders so large they could devour a hummingbird. A century and a half before Darwin wrote *The Origin of Species*, Maria vividly showed nature as a struggle for survival.

In the process of collecting, painting, and frantically making notes, Maria began to feel dizzy and exhausted. Her head ached, her body flushed hot to cold. Was this one of the dreaded tropical fevers? She was fifty-two, after all, considered elderly in a time when life expectancies hovered around forty years old. Vigorous and almost unstoppable her whole life, this illness hit her hard.

Nonetheless, desperate to keep exploring, and realizing she would never again have this opportunity, Maria pressed on, raising more species, checking her findings, sketching and recording every transformation in her study book. More than anything, she wished to trace the path of each marvelous creature, from egg—laid on a particular host plant—to larva, to pupa, to adult. She wanted to prove her hunch: that even these exotic creatures followed the same cycle as the European caterpillars she had already studied so thoroughly.

Driven by a sense of urgency, she soon ventured beyond Paramaribo, hiring workers to hack through dense underbrush. She and Dorothea journeyed far upstream to La Providence, the former Labadist outpost where Cornelis van Sommelsdijk had collected the specimens Maria had seen at Waltha Castle. Though a number of Labadists still lived at La Providence, the plantation was eerily quiet, a bleak reminder of the dangers of colonial life. Van Sommelsdijk had been killed by his own troops several years before, and many of his slaves had vanished into the jungle.

A white witch moth (*Thysania agrippina*) in a South American rainforest, showing its huge eleven-inch wingspan.

Maria's depiction of the white witch moth on a gummi-gutta tree (oozing yellow resin) with caterpillar and cocoon.

> *"The heat in this country is staggering, so that one can do no work at all without great difficulty, and I myself nearly paid for it with my death, which is why I could not stay there longer."* — M.M.

On a tree nearby, Maria discovered an enormous striped caterpillar. She carefully tended it, and weeks later, a huge, delicately patterned gray-and-white moth emerged from the pupa, the biggest she had ever seen. Natives called it "Ghost Moth" or "White Witch." Its wings dwarfed Maria's outstretched hand.

There were so many wonders here! Huge beetles with whiplike antennae! Box-shaped caterpillars with spiderlike legs! Pupae like tiny carved jewels! Weary, ill, and frazzled with the heat, Maria scrambled to gather and paint as many as she could, with Dorothea's help.

Maria would have packed specimens like this lantern fly (*Fulgora laternaria*) carefully for shipboard travel, so that she could show them to colleagues in Amsterdam and use them as models for painting.

Maria had hoped to remain in Surinam long enough to confirm all her discoveries, to repeat them and check her data as she had always done in Europe. As her fevers grew worse, however, she realized she would not last another full growing season.

After only twenty-one months, she reluctantly gathered up all the bits and pieces of their research: the notebooks full of sketches; the pinned beetles, butterflies, and moths; the seeds, bulbs, and carefully pressed flowers of tropical plants. She and Dorothea hastily preserved caterpillars and reptiles in brandy and packed up live cocoons and lizard eggs in the hope these might hatch during the months at sea.

On June 18, 1701, Maria and Dorothea boarded the Dutch ship *De Vreede* (the Peace). Though exhausted, ill, and anxious about the voyage ahead, they carried evidence of a vast, teeming, interconnected ecosystem of plants and insects, the likes of which the great European academies had never seen.

I need only find
that sweet
stem, that perfect leaf
to deposit my pearls,
before I fold
at last
these tattered
wings.

A butterfly laying an egg on a leaf.

Chapter 12: EGG

1701 Amsterdam, the Netherlands

By the time *De Vreede* reached Amsterdam, Maria needed rest and care. Instead, spurred by her irrepressible enthusiasm, she invited friends and colleagues to view her precious Surinam sketches and specimens, which she had "dried and well displayed in boxes where they can be seen by all."

Everyone who visited said the same thing: *The world needs to see this.*

Publication was a daunting prospect, however. Creating a book would take years, and there was no certainty she would sell enough copies to finance the project.

> *"A number of nature lovers . . . strongly urged me to have them printed. They were of the opinion that these were the first and most unusual drawings ever painted in America. The expenses associated with carrying out this work frightened me at first, but then I finally made up my mind to do it anyway."* — M.M.

As she had done so many times before, Maria turned to her daughters for help. Dorothea, who had married the ship's surgeon Philip Hendriks shortly after returning to Amsterdam, invited her mother to come live with them. The two women set up a studio there, aided by elder daughter Johanna, who soon afterward headed to Surinam herself. While her husband administered the Orphans Board (which kept track of Dutch orphans in Paramaribo), Johanna sent back insect sketches and specimens whenever possible.

Maria envisioned a big book—bigger than her earlier caterpillar books—emblazoned with prints of life-size Surinam marvels. She wanted to fill the pages with color, to dazzle her readers as she herself had been dazzled.

First, however, she had to weave together all she had seen. She leafed through her study book, crammed with sketches of insects painted from life on scraps of vellum. She sorted trays of dried, pinned butterflies and bottles of pupae preserved in brandy. She fingered dried plants, pressed between paper to preserve fine details. Packed hurriedly in those last grueling weeks in Surinam, much of this material had been jumbled together, and some did not survive the voyage intact.

Could she fill in the gaps? Whom could she consult if she was uncertain? An old colleague, Caspar Commelin, director of Amsterdam's Botanical Garden, agreed to identify many of the tropical plants and provide their Latin names. Maria was on her own when it came to the insects, however. She was the only naturalist in Europe who had set eyes on most of them. This was pioneering work. She would have to rely on her sharp memory, her knowledge of insects, and her detailed notes.

Though she did not know the scientific names of her insects—these species were unknown in Europe—she decided she did not really care. Others could argue over names and classifications. She simply wanted to capture these small communities of insects and plants interacting with one another, just as she had witnessed them.

"Because the modern world is very picky and the scholars have different opinions, I simply stayed with my own observations." —M.M.

She chose a young, growing pineapple for the first page of her Surinam book—the most recognizable of all her plants. She wanted to welcome the reader into this strange world. But in a nod to the wildness of the place, she added huge tropical cockroaches on the pineapple's scaly leaves and described its molting process in her text: "When they [the cockroach larvae] have reached their full size, the skin on their back cracks open, and out crawls a winged cockroach that is soft and white. The skin remains lying there as though it were the cockroach, but it is empty inside."

In painting after painting, she pieced together the stages of all these strange lives. She matched each caterpillar with its host plant—the one it was eating when she found it. She combined images of its egg, larval stage, its pupa, and the butterfly or moth that "crept from" the chrysalis or cocoon. Any other insects she found nearby, such as flies, wasps, or beetles, she also included as part of its plant-insect community. A few of the later plates even showed, for the first time, the life cycles of tropical frogs and toads, as well as lizards and snakes. All in all, she created sixty life-size scenes, depicting ninety new insect metamorphoses and fifty-three species of plants.

Still weak from her tropical illness and pressed for time, she was forced to hire others to etch and engrave most of the copper plates based on her paintings. Though chronically low on funds, she chose Amsterdam's best professional engravers. This book was too important to scrimp on details.

In this first illustration from her new book, *Metamorphosis insectorum Surinamensium*, Maria shows a pineapple plant that has just flowered and is developing fruit. On the right are perched the nymph and adult stages of a tropical cockroach, which she described as "the most infamous of all insects in America because of the great harm they bring to all who live there, inasmuch as they ruin wool, linen, food, and drinks."

A. To create her magnificent new book, *Metamorphosis insectorum Surinamensium*, Maria took elements from the studies she painted in Surinam and produced complex full-page designs in watercolors. In this composition for Plate 11, she includes several instars of the giant silk moth caterpillar, the pupa, and both front and back of the adult moth (*Arsenura armida*) perched on a palisade tree.

B. Her full-page compositions were then engraved onto copper plates, printed in black-and-white, and bound into books with her text. Some books were sold like this, with uncolored prints, while others were colored by hand.

C. Some prints, with ink still wet, were pressed to fresh
vellum, transferring a reverse image onto the vellum.
This "counterproof," with its softer ink outlines, was then
colored by hand.

"I hope I shall have completed the entire work by next January, provided God grants me and the engravers life and health. . . . Patience is a beneficial little herb." —M.M.

Published in 1705 in both Dutch and Latin editions, and measuring an impressive twenty-two inches high, *Metamorphosis insectorum Surinamensium* (The metamorphosis of the insects of Surinam) was a huge, gorgeous book—a masterpiece. In the style of the time, it had a lengthy subtitle: *Wherein the Surinamese caterpillars and worms are displayed in all their transformations, described from life on the plants, flowers, and fruit where they were found. There are also frogs, amazing toads, lizards, snakes, spiders, and ants shown and explained, and everything was painted and written in America, first-hand and life-size by Maria Sibylla Merian.*

For many, it was the first glimpse into a completely unknown, extraordinary world. Reviews praised "the great passion for investigation and tireless diligence of this woman," and wealthy collectors immediately snapped up the more expensive copies, which had been hand-colored in Maria's workshop. While scholars preferred the Latin edition (Latin being the language of science), fellow "nature lovers" pored over Maria's Dutch edition, full of her simple, vivid descriptions: "The [banana] blossom is a very lovely flower with five blood red leaves as thick as leather and covered on the underside with blue dew."

OPPOSITE: Plate 12 from *Metamorphosis insectorum Surinamensium*, showing a banana flower and young bananas. Maria also includes a saturniid moth with its caterpillar, cocoon, and pupa.

P. Sluyter Sculp

But the new book was not just an exquisite work of art. It made a bold scientific declaration: even in the mysterious jungles of the New World, toads did not spring from mud, leaves did not change into moths, or butterflies into birds. Each creature progressed through its own stages of transformation.

In an unprecedented acknowledgment of Maria's experiment-based research, the Royal Society of London, a famed scientific group (which would not admit women to its membership for another 250 years), mentioned her in their publication *Philosophical Transactions:* "That Curious Person Madam Maria Sibilla Merian . . . being lately returned from

Even in this dramatic composition *Spectacled Caiman and a False Coral Snake* (published in a later edition of the Surinam book), Maria shows the signs of a dedicated naturalist. Under one of the adult caiman's rear legs, a baby caiman hatches from its egg, and to the left is a coral snake egg. Maria wanted to know—and to share—the origin of all creatures, not just butterflies.

Black-Billed Cuckoo, from John J. Audubon's *Birds of America,* published in 1827, nearly 125 years after Maria's work, shows her influence on this artist-naturalist. Audubon paints an active cuckoo pair within a community of other species, reaching to grasp a beetle on a magnolia bush in its native Louisiana. Not being quite as particular as Maria about setting, he does admit in his description that the birds neither eat the bugs depicted nor frequent the magnolia bush, but rather eat shellfish in a marsh setting.

Surinam in the West Indies doth now ... publish a Curious History of all those Insects and their transmutations that she hath there observed, which are many and very rare."

Maria's beautiful, accessible art and text electrified her fellow naturalists. Most of the species she discovered were unknown to Europeans at the time, and her observations were widely quoted and discussed. In the years that followed, inspired by her work, other European artist-naturalists such as Mark Catesby and, later, John James Audubon journeyed to the Americas and published their findings, modeling their illustrations on her unique style of placing organisms within their ecological environment.

While working on her Surinam book, Maria painted a beautiful series of seashells on commission to bolster her dwindling funds. They were eventually used in naturalist Georgius Rumphius's 1705 book, *The Ambonese Curiosity Cabinet.*

Despite Maria's high hopes, *Metamorphosis insectorum Surinamensium* did not make much money for her. Having spared no expense on the quality of paper and engraving, she barely recovered the costs of the first printing.

She had worked at such a feverish pace to produce this monumental book that she was tired. Money worries were ever constant, and she was no longer young. Still, life had always been a series of passions, obstacles, and surprises for Maria Merian.

Soon her fingers began to itch for the feel of cocoons, her eyes to dart about for the flutter of wings. She might never again travel quite so far, but she could still turn her profound and unwavering focus to the gardens just outside her window.

Caterpillars awaited: growing, shifting, transforming. She would be ready with paintbrush and sketchbook to record their complex, miraculous lives.

"When I saw this large moth, quite well-adorned by nature, for the first time many years ago, I could not cease to be amazed at its beautiful shadowing and alternating colors. . . . It took me a very long time [to successfully raise another. . . . Thus when . . . this pretty moth-bird actually appeared . . . I was so filled with joy, and so content in my desire that I cannot describe it enough." — M.M.

The Woman in Her World

Maria Sibylla Merian recorded her last research entry in the spring of 1711.

Never truly recovered from the tropical illness contracted in Surinam—probably malaria—she suffered a stroke in 1715 and died two years later, at the age of sixty-nine.

Although the first edition of *Metamorphosis insectorum Surinamensium* had not sold widely, later editions in French and Latin spread her work throughout Europe. On the very day of her death, an agent of Tsar Peter the Great bought a collection of almost three hundred of her original watercolors to help found Russia's first art museum.

Carl Linnaeus, who developed the Latin system for naming organisms that we still use today, relied heavily on Maria's insect discoveries in his 1758 book *Systema Naturae* (tenth edition), citing her more than 130 times. All in all, Linnaeus and his followers used Maria's work—in both Surinam and Europe—to identify at least one hundred species.

Maria's pioneering exploration offended many gentleman scholars at the time, however. One critic insisted she could not have gone to Surinam alone and must have been accompanied by her husband (even though Maria was unmarried at the time). One took offense at her inclusion of native lore: "The grand defect of the work is the introduction of idle stories related to her by strangers." Others criticized her lack of insect classification and the seemingly haphazard organization of her books. Later editions of her Surinam book were needlessly reorganized according to different classification systems, garbling and misrepresenting her find-

This portrait of Maria Sibylla Merian, which appeared on the German five-hundred-Deutschmark bill, is based on the only verified engraving of her.

ings. While some great naturalists still praised her books, she fell into disfavor with a scientific establishment that increasingly rejected the work of self-taught amateurs. Around this time—1834—the word *scientist* was first coined, beginning an era that gradually professionalized the study of the natural world, and began to divide it into ever more specialized fields.

Maria's three European caterpillar books (the last one published by her younger daughter after Maria's death) are models of scientific accuracy, but her *Metamorphosis insectorum Surinamensium* does contain some errors—as did many scientific works of the time—mostly due to the extreme conditions under which she collected her data. In some plates, caterpillars and pupae are shown with the wrong adults. A few scenes appear to be combinations of her own observations and faulty information collected from others. In most cases, however, her paintings are so precise and lifelike that even today they could be used as a field guide to European and Surinamese insects. In fact, some scientists believe that Maria

Plate 59 from the Surinam book shows the common Surinamese toad (*Pipa pipa*). Maria was the first to document the life stages of this unusual amphibian, which attaches its eggs to its back. She had planned a second Surinam book with illustrations of other amphibians and reptiles, but could not manage it financially.

At least six plants, nine butterflies, a moth (*Erinnyis merianae*), a toad (*Rhinella merianae*), and a large South American lizard called a black tegu (*Tupinambis merianae*), pictured above, have been named after Maria by later scientists.

may have been the only person to record the metamorphoses of many species in Surinam that have since become extinct.

Fortunately, today's scientists, historians, and art collectors have rediscovered and acknowledged her work for what it is: amazingly beautiful, accurate portrayals of insect metamorphoses and ecosystems. Her words and artwork told fascinating, intertwined stories to a public still

Maria's artwork has been used through the centuries in many different ways. This U.S. stamp is based on a tulip from her flower book. (Author's collection)

highly suspicious of insects. At a time when most scholars were trying to separate the natural world into categories, Maria insisted on finding connections—between life stages, between insect and plant, between art and science. The great German writer and statesman Johann Wolfgang von Goethe later marveled at how easily she moved back and forth between art and science, between the "inspection of nature and the aims of painting." The noted naturalist Sir David Attenborough considers her one of the most adventurous and distinctive artists of her time.

Why did Maria insist on painting her insects with the plants they favored? Why was she so obsessively thorough in her documentation? Maybe years of meticulous fieldwork—rather than years of classical education—allowed her to observe more keenly. Maybe, as an outsider, she could see a bigger picture, take more risks. Maybe she was sending a message ahead to the future. Living creatures exist with one another in a delicate balance, she seemed to be saying. The word *ecology* was not invented until more than fifty years after her death, but once again, Maria was ahead of her time. Many have called her the world's first ecologist.

Even more than her magnificent art, this was her legacy. She saw nature as an ever-transforming web of connections—and changed our view of it forever.

"It has often happened that the rarest and most beautiful caterpillars change into the simplest creatures, and the simplest caterpillars become the most beautiful moths and butterflies." —M.M.

On the last page of her Surinam book Maria painted the beautiful giant owl butterfly (*Caligo idomeneus*) with its caterpillar and chrysalis. She also included the humble brown wasp (*Hymenoptera*), considered by many a pest, but which she admired for its ingeniously constructed nest.

AUTHOR'S NOTE

What made me—a poet—tackle the biography of a little-known seventeenth-century German naturalist? I was drawn to Maria's intricate Surinam prints the first time I saw them at the Minneapolis Institute of Art, and captivated with the details of her life. Then a friend unexpectedly sent me several Cecropia moth cocoons, which bloomed into gorgeously huge, furry moths. The project truly took hold, however, when I finally found a translation of Maria's Surinam notes. The plainspoken intensity of her voice propelled me to tell her story.

In many ways, Maria was an enigma. She rarely wrote of anything but caterpillars, leaving me to wonder how she felt about her childhood, her husband, her daughters, her move to Waltha. In fact, the story of her life is still changing with new scholarship. What we do know is that she had boundless energy, insatiable curiosity, and superhuman focus—traits that might have been difficult to live with, but ones that marked her as a true scientist at a time when the odds were stacked against her. Like other intrepid field biologists who even today continue her groundbreaking work, she always followed the mystery—while remaining a bit of a mystery herself.

Wanting to follow in Maria's footsteps, I, too, raised caterpillars while writing this book. I chose a species native to both the United States and Germany, the painted lady (*Vanessa cardui*). I even planted hollyhocks—this butterfly's host plant—in my garden to feed them. Armed with a camera and a vast digital archive of information, I had a much different research experience than Maria. Even so, there were times I felt very close to her: when a pupa wiggled in my hand, startling me as one had startled her. Or when after hours of waiting for the pupae to eclose, I discovered that every single butterfly had, in turn, slipped from its chrysalis as soon as I left the room. I never did see one emerge. What patience it must have taken Maria to wait for each stage of metamorphosis!

As I prepared to release my adult butterflies, my five-year-old neighbor stopped by. "Can I help?" she asked, intrigued. The butterflies' feet tickled her hand as she let them go. "I love this," she said fervently as the last one drifted out of view. At that moment, I felt Maria's bright spirit passing from one generation to the next.

TIMELINE

1640s

1647   Maria is born April 2 in Frankfurt, Germany, daughter of Johanna Sibylla Heim and Matthäus (*Me-tay-os*) Merian the Elder.

1648   The Thirty Years' War ends, one of the longest and most destructive conflicts in European history. Between war and disease, the German population has been cut in half since 1618.

        European colonization of the "New World" (the Americas) is fully under way, with merchant ships sailing back and forth across the Atlantic.

1650s

1650   Maria's father dies.

1651   Maria's mother marries the still-life painter Jacob Marrel. Over the next decade, he teaches Maria how to paint.

1660s

1660   Maria begins to raise and study silkworms at age thirteen.

        The Royal Society, an academy of "natural philosophers," is founded in England with the motto *Nullius in verba,* or "Take nobody's word for it."

By this date, over 20,000 women have been tried and executed as witches in Germany alone.

1662   Johannes Goedart (*Hude-hart*) publishes *Metamorphosis naturalis Insectorum,* depicting caterpillars and the adult butterflies that develop from them.

1664   The Dutch government trades New Amsterdam (later New York) to the British for the territory of Surinam in South America.

1665   Maria marries the artist and publisher Johann Andreas Graff (*Grawf*).

An outbreak of the Black Death (bubonic plague) threatens London and other European cities, killing an estimated 100,000 people.

1668   Maria's first child, Johanna Helena, is born.

The Italian scholar Francesco Redi (*Red-ee*) demonstrates that maggots come from the eggs of flies. A year later, Jan Swammerdam (*Shwum-er-dum*), a Dutchman, argues that insects develop through various stages in the same gradual manner as other animals.

1670s

1670   Maria and her family move to Nuremberg, Germany, and establish a print studio and publishing house.

1675   At age twenty-eight, Maria publishes the first volume of *Neues Blumenbuch* (New book of flowers) after beginning to teach painting techniques to her "company of maidens."

Antonie van Leeuwenhoek (*Lay*-ven-who-k) discovers bacteria and microscopic animals (protozoa).

1678   Maria's second child, Dorothea (Dor-o-*tay*-a) Maria Henriette, is born.

1679   Maria publishes the first volume of *Der Raupen wunderbare Verwandelung, und sonderbare Blumen-nahrung* (The wondrous transformation of caterpillars and their particular nourishment from flowers), her study of European caterpillars.

1680s

1681   Maria's stepfather dies, and she and her daughters move back to Frankfurt to help manage her mother's estate.

1683   Volume two of Maria's caterpillar transformation book is published in Frankfurt.

1685   Maria separates from her husband and travels to Waltha (*Vawl*-ta) Castle in the Netherlands with her mother and two daughters to join a Labadist community.

1687   Sir Isaac Newton publishes his theory of gravity.

1690s

1691　Maria leaves the Labadist community and moves with her daughters to Amsterdam.

1692　Maria's husband files for divorce.

　　　The Salem witch trials begin in the Massachusetts Bay Colony, resulting in the executions of twenty people, fourteen of them women.

1699　Maria embarks for Surinam with her daughter Dorothea in June.

1700s

1701　Maria and Dorothea return from Surinam.

1705　*Metamorphosis insectorum Surinamensium* (The metamorphosis of the insects of Surinam) is published.

1710s

1715　Maria suffers a stroke.

1717　Maria dies on January 13 in Amsterdam at age sixty-nine. Tsar Peter the Great buys a collection of her watercolors for his "art cabinet" in St. Petersburg, Russia.

1718   Dorothea completes and publishes volume three of *Der Raupen wunderbare Verwandelung*.

A combined edition of all three of Maria's European caterpillar books, with text condensed and translated into Latin, is published as *Erucarum Ortus* (Origin of caterpillars).

1719   *Metamorphosis insectorum Surinamensium* is reprinted in Dutch and Latin, using Maria's sixty original illustrations, plus twelve more she had hoped to include in another volume.

Dorothea and her husband move to St. Petersburg to help Peter the Great organize his art cabinet, which becomes one of the world's first art museums. Dorothea teaches botanical and insect drawing in St. Petersburg to a new generation of artist-naturalists.

1730   A French edition of *Erucarum Ortus* is published (*Histoire des Insectes de l'Europe*), which will later be used by Carl Linnaeus to classify and name more than one hundred insects—names we still use today.

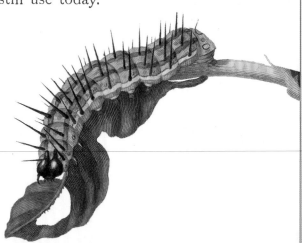

Quote Sources

2. Hatching

12   *"every flying creeping thing . . .":* Leviticus 11:41–43, Hoyt, *Insect Lives,*
        p. 35.

        "From youth on . . .": Fuegi, *MIS* translation.

3. First Instar

16   *"I was always encouraged . . .":* Wettengl, *Maria Sibylla Merian,* p. 58.

4. Second Instar

22   *"Because almost everyone is . . .":* Beer, *Butterflies, Beetles and Other Insects,*
        notes translated by author, p. 141.

24   *"You must take great pains . . .":* Ibid.

25   *"When the moth wants . . .":* Ibid.

5. Third Instar

29   *"These caterpillars are by nature . . .":* Ibid., p. 143.

33   *"I make mention in the following of nothing . . .":* Wettengl, *Maria Sibylla
        Merian,* p. 159.

6. Fourth Instar

36   *"company of maidens":* Wettengl, *Maria Sibylla Merian,* p. 262.

        "to copy and paint, and to sew . . .": NB, p. 84.

38   *"the daughter of the famous engraver . . .":* Stearn and Rücker, *MIS,* p. 2.

39   *"noxious animals":* Pieters and Winthagen, "Maria Sibylla Merian,"
        p. 13.

        "gets entangled in the endless objects . . .": Pieters and Winthagen, "Maria
        Sibylla Merian," p. 13.

40   *"When put on the warm hand . . .":* Todd, *Chrysalis,* p. 60.

91   *"The Indians put its . . .":* Fuegi, *MIS*, plate 10.

       "Whenever it is grilled . . .": Ibid., plate 16.

       "string [musk seeds] on . . .": Ibid., plate 42.

       "the Indians draw . . .": Ibid., plate 44.

       "like the feathers . . .": Ibid., plate 3.

94   *"One day I wandered . . .":* Attenborough, *Amazing Rare Things*, p. 148.

95   *"as if one had mixed . . .":* Fuegi, *MIS*, plate 2.

96   *"People there do not . . .":* Ibid., plate 36.

       "We opened [a box] with astonishment . . .": Ibid., plate 49.

       "clean as the handle of a broom": Ibid., plate 18.

101   *"The heat in this country . . .":* Wettengl, *Maria Sibylla Merian*, p. 264.

12. Egg

103   *"dried and well displayed in boxes . . .":* Ibid.

104   *"A number of nature lovers . . .":* Fuegi, *MIS*, Introduction.

105   *"Because the modern world . . .":* Ibid.

106   *"When they . . .":* Ibid., plate 49.

107   *"the most infamous of all insects . . .":* Ibid., plate 1.

110   *"I hope I shall . . .":* Wettengl, *Maria Sibylla Merian*, p. 264.

      "the great passion . . .": Todd, *Chrysalis*, p. 216.

      "The [banana] blossom . . .": Fuegi, *MIS*, plate 12.

112   *"That Curious Person . . .":* Royal Society, *Philosophical Transactions*, p. 18.

115   *"When I saw this large moth . . .":* Wettengl, *Maria Sibylla Merian*, p. 62.

The Woman in Her World

116   *"The grand defect . . .":* Guilding, "Observations on the Work," p. 356.

120   *"inspection of nature . . .":* Bürger, Epilogue to *NB*, p. 93.

      "It has often happened . . .": Fuegi, *MIS*, plate 12.

Selected Bibliography

Original works by Maria Sibylla Merian

NB   *Neues Blumenbuch* (New book of flowers). 3 vols. Nuremberg: Johann Andreas Graff, 1675–80.

DRWV   *Der Raupen wunderbare Verwandelung, und sonderbare Blumen-nahrung* (The wondrous transformation of caterpillars and their particular nourishment from flowers). 3 vols. Nuremberg and Frankfurt, 1679, 1683, and 1718.

MIS   *Metamorphosis insectorum Surinamensium* (The metamorphosis of the insects of Surinam). Amsterdam: G. Valck, 1705. Published in Latin and Dutch. A later edition appeared in 1719 with new plates, published by Johannes Oosterwukin Amsterdam.

Facsimiles of works by Maria Sibylla Merian

Beer, Wolf-Dietrich, ed. *Butterflies, Beetles and Other Insects: The Leningrad Book of Notes and Studies.* New York: McGraw Hill, 1976.

Bürger, Thomas. Epilogue to *NB*. Munich and New York: Prestel Verlag, 1999.

Fuegi, John. Unpublished translation of *MIS,* 2006.

Hollmann, Eckhard (edited and introduction by), and Wolf-Dietrich Beer (commentary by). *The St. Petersburg Watercolours.* Berlin: Prestel Verlag, 2003.

Schmidt-Loske, Katharina. Commentary on plates from *MIS*. Cologne: Taschen, 2009.

Stearn, William T. Introduction to *The Wondrous Transformation of Caterpillars: Fifty Engravings Selected from* Erucarum Ortus. London: Scolar Press, 1978.

Stearn, W. T., and E. Rücker. Commentary on facsimile edition of *MIS*. London: Pion, 1980.

Ullman, Ernst, ed. *The Leningrad Watercolours*. New York: Harcourt Brace Jovanovich, A Helen and Kurt Wolf Book, 1974.

Works by others

Alexander, Michael, ed. *Discovering the New World, Based on the Works of Theodore de Bry*. New York: Harper & Row, 1976.

Aristotle. *Generation of Animals* (originally published 350 B.C.). Translated by A. L. Peck. Cambridge: Harvard University Press, 1963.

Attenborough, David, ed. *Amazing Rare Things: The Art of Natural History in the Age of Discovery*. New Haven: Yale University Press, 2007.

Beatty, Noelle. *Suriname*. New York: Chelsea House, 1999.

Benson, Richard. *The Printed Picture*. New York: Museum of Modern Art, 2008.

Brafman, David, and Stephanie Schrader. *Insects and Flowers: The Art of Maria Sibylla Merian*. Los Angeles: J. Paul Getty Museum, 2008.

Briggs, Robin. *Witches and Neighbors: The Social and Cultural Context of European Witchcraft*. New York: Viking, 1996.

Davis, N. Z. *Women on the Margins: Three Seventeenth-Century Lives*. Cambridge: Harvard University Press, 1995.

Essig, E. O. *A History of Entomology* (facsimile of the 1931 edition). New York: Hafner, 1972.

Etheridge, Kay. "Maria Sibylla Merian and the Metamorphosis of Natural History." *Endeavor* 35, no. 1 (2010): 15–21.

———. "Maria Sibylla Merian: The First Ecologist?" In *Women and Science, Seventeenth Century to Present: Pioneers, Activists and Protagonists*, edited by Donna Andreolle and Veronique Molinari. 35–54. Newcastle on Tyne: Cambridge Scholars Publishing, 2011.

———. "Maria Sibylla Merian's Frogs." *Bibliotheca Herpetologica* 8, no. 2 (2010): 20–27.

———. *The Flowering of Ecology: Maria Sibylla Merian's Caterpillar Book.* Boston: Brill, forthcoming.

Etheridge, Kay, and Florence Pieters. "Maria Sibylla Merian: Pioneering Naturalist, Artist, and Inspiration for Catesby." In *The Curious Mr. Catesby,* edited by E. Charles Nelson and David J. Elliott. Athens: University of Georgia Press, 2015.

Fuegi, John, and Jo Francis. Email, January 31, 2017.

Griffiths, Antony. *Prints and Printmaking.* Berkeley: University of California Press, 1966.

Guilding, Landsdown. "Observations on the Work of Maria Sibylla Merian," *Magazine of Natural History,* vol. 7 (1834) 355–75.

Hoyt, Erich and Ted Schultz, ed. *Insect Lives.* Toronto: Wiley & Sons. 1999.

Kelps-Hok, Patricia. *Search for Sibylla: The Seventeenth Century's Woman of Today.* Bloomington, Ind.: Xlibris, 2007.

Linnaeus, Carl. *Systema naturae* (10th edition). Stockholm: L. Salvius, 1758.

Marshall, Sherrin, ed. *Women in Reformation and Counter-Reformation Europe: Private and Public Worlds.* Bloomington: Indiana University Press, 1989.

Maxwell-Stuart, P. G. *Witchcraft in Europe and the New World, 1400–1800.* New York: Palgrave, 2001.

Muffet, Thomas. *The History of Four-Footed Beasts and Serpents and Insects* (facsimile of the 1658 edition). New York: Da Capo Press, 1967.

Neri, Janice. *The Insect and the Image: Visualizing Nature in Early Modern Europe, 1500–1700.* Minneapolis: University of Minnesota Press, 2011.

Paravisini-Gebert, Lizabeth. "Maria Sibylla Merian: The Dawn of Field Ecology in the Forests of Suriname, 1699–1701." *Review: Literature and Arts of the Americas* 45, no. 1 (2012): 10–20.

Philosophical Transactions of the Royal Society, vol. 23 (1703–4), 1–22.

Pick, Cecilia Mary. "Rhetoric of the Author Presentation: The Case of Maria

Sibylla Merian." Ph.D. diss., University of Texas, 2004.

Pieters, Florence, and Diny Winthagen. "Maria Sibylla Merian, Naturalist and Artist." *Archives of Natural History* 26, no. 1 (1999): 1–18.

Reitsma, Ella. *Maria Sibylla Merian and Daughters: Women of Art and Science.* Amsterdam: Rembrandt House Museum and J. Paul Getty Museum, 2008.

Roeck, Bernd. *Civic Culture and Everyday Life in Early Modern Germany.* Boston: Brill, 2006.

Saxby, T. J. *The Quest for the New Jerusalem: Jean Labadie and the Labadists, 1610–1744.* Boston: Martinus Nijhoff, 1987.

Schrader, Stephanie, Nancy Turner, and Nancy Yocco. "Naturalism Under the Microscope: A Technical Study of the Insects of Surinam." *Getty Research Journal*, no. 4 (2012): 161–72.

Stijnman, Ad. *Engraving and Etching 1400–2000.* London: Archetype Publications, 2012.

Todd, Kim. *Chrysalis: Maria Sibylla Merian and the Secrets of Metamorphosis.* New York: Harcourt, 2007.

Wettengl, Kurt, ed. *Maria Sibylla Merian, 1647–1717: Artist and Naturalist.* Frankfurt: Hatje Cantz Verlag, 1998.

Wunder, Heide. *He Is the Sun, She Is the Moon: Women in Early Modern Germany.* Cambridge: Harvard University Press, 1998.

FOR FURTHER READING

Finding Wonders: Three Girls Who Changed Science, by Jeannine
    Atkins. New York: Atheneum, 2016.
A Butterfly Journey: Maria Sibylla Merian, Artist and Scientist, by
    Boris Friedewald. New York: Prestel, 2015.
Maria Merian's Butterflies, by Kate Heard. London: Royal
    Collection Trust, 2016.

AND FOR YOUNGER READERS

Summer Birds: The Butterflies of Maria Merian, by Margarita
    Engle; illustrated by Julie Paschkis. New York:
    Henry Holt, 2010.

Acknowledgments

I am profoundly grateful to all who helped me on this long and infinitely rewarding journey, especially the many Merian scholars who made sure her legacy was not forgotten. John Fuegi and Jo Francis, producers of *Out of the Chrysalis: A Portrait of Maria Sibylla Merian* (Flare Films) generously lent me their advice and their translation of Maria's words. Professor Kay Etheridge of Gettysburg College steered me toward valuable sources and answered innumerable questions. Florence Pieters, former curator of Artis Library at the University of Amsterdam, read an early copy of the manuscript for accuracy, boosting my confidence immeasurably. The Minneapolis Institute of Art kindly allowed me free use of their digital holdings. Librarians at the University of Minnesota's Andersen Horticultural Library and Wangensteen Historical Library of Biology and Medicine enabled me to see and touch Maria's books for the first time. And the UMSP Entomology Department allowed me to view and photograph their extensive insect collection.

Deepest thanks, always, to my sisters-in-revision: Michelle Lackner, Tracy Maurer, Tunie Munson-Benson, and Laura Purdie Salas; and to early reader Julie Reimer, who gave me a child's-eye view. Thanks also to Julie Hahnke, for those amazing cecropia cocoons. Eli Sidman, Gabriel Sidman, and Marta Bueno Martín read many drafts and cheered me on at every stage. My husband, Jim, believed in Maria's story from the very start, offering wise advice, editorial help, and great patience in fielding my worries and uncertainty.

My heartfelt gratitude to everyone at Houghton Mifflin Harcourt, including Betsy Groban, Mary Wilcox, Karen Walsh, Linda Magram, Lisa DiSarro, Mary Magrisso, Margaret Anne Miles, and Alison Kerr Miller. The editorial assistant Lily Kessinger provided excellent comments on the text and great help thereafter, and the senior designer Rebecca Bond brought my manuscript to life with her beautiful book design. Finally, to my editor, Ann Rider, dear friend and mentor, who allowed me to expand the narrative instead of contract it—thank you for believing that, as Maria would say, sometimes "the simplest caterpillars can become the most beautiful moths and butterflies."

IMAGE CREDITS

Images by Maria Sibylla Merian

Courtesy of the Minnich Collection, the Ethel Morrison Van Derlip Fund, 1966, Minneapolis Institute of Art, Minneapolis, Minnesota, Photos © Minneapolis Institute of Art

i,v, 102: "Bananas and Blue Lizard," c. 1705, hand-colored etching and engraving, P.18,720

vi, 6, 44, 96 (detail), **108**: "Caterpillars, Butterflies, and Flower," c. 1705, etching and engraving, P.18,716

vii, 38 (detail): "Blue Butterflies and Red Larva, Blue Spines," c. 1705, hand-colored etching and engraving, P.18,728

71, 126, 127 (detail): "Metamorphosis of a Frog and Blue Flower," 17th cen., watercolor, 66.25.171

100: "Moths, Caterpillars, and Foliage," c. 1705, hand-colored etching and engraving, P.18.719

111: "Inflorescence of Banana," c. 1705, hand-colored etching and engraving, P.18,718

118: "Male Suriname Toad with Eggs on Back, Shells, and Flowering Plant," c. 1705, hand-colored etching and engraving, P.18.727

University Library Johann Christian Senckenberg, Frankfurt/Main, Germany

15: "17 Original Drawings of Plants and Animals," 1669, ink drawing with chalk

52, 136: "Frontispiece from *Der Raupen wunderbare Verwandelung*," hand-colored engraving, 1679

Courtesy of the Getty Research Institute Digital Collections Open Content Program, Los Angeles, CA

From *De Europische insecten,* all hand-colored engravings, 1730:

20, 54 (detail): "Brandenetelbladeren"

28, 76: "Wonderbare Rupsen"

58 (detail): "Hyacinth"

64 (detail): "Druivenblossem"

From *MIS*, all hand-colored transfer engravings, 1719:

12, 84 (detail), **97, 101** (detail): "Double-blossomed pomegranate with lantern flies and cicada," Plate 49

40, 89,140 (detail): "Belly-ache bush with giant sphinx moth"

73, 128 (detail): "Blue morpho butterfly, larva and pupa"

98: "Branch of a guava tree with leaf-cutter ants, army ants, spiders, and hummingbird," Plate 18

105 (detail): "Branch of sweet orange tree with Rothschildia hesperus moth"

109: "Branch of a swamp immortelle and Saturniid moth," Plate 11

112: "Surinam caiman biting South American false coral snake"

Archive of the Russian Academy of Sciences, St. Petersburg, Russia

All images watercolor and gouache on parchment

23 (detail): "Tarantula, Mantids and Beetles," c. 1699, IX. Op. 8. D. L. 63. 1

42 (detail): "Beetles and Larvae," all c. 1699, IX. Op. 8. D. 59. L. 1

63: "Fennel, Dill, and Swallowtail," c. 1688, IX. Op. 8. D. 1. 24. A

66: "Beetle, Moths and Fern," c. 1688, IX. Op. 8. D. L. 20. 1

92: "Butterflies, Moths, Treehopper, and Flannel Moth Caterpillar," c. 1699, IX. Op. 8. D. L. 56. 1

93: "Tarantula, Mantids and Beetles," c. 1699, IX. Op. 8. D. L. 63. 1

114: "Sea Snails and Turbo Shells," c. 1704, IX. Op. 8. D. L. 74. 1

121: "Giant Atlas and Wild Wasp," c. 1700, IX. Op. 8. D. 29. L. 1

Flowers, Butterflies and Insects: All 154 Engravings from Erucarum Ortus, Dover Publications, © 1991 and 2005

26, 124, 125: "Silkmoths"

51: "Garden Tiger on Hyacinth Flower"

57: "Tussock Moth on Dandelion"

Alamy.com

49, 95, 138 (detail): Papaya

Courtesy of the National Museum of Women in the Arts, Washington, D.C.; Gift of Wallace and Wilhelmina Holladay

107: "Plate 1 from *Dissertation in Insect Generations and Metamorphosis in Surinam,* 2nd ed., 1719," hand-colored engraving on paper. Photo by Lee Stalsworth.

Courtesy of The British Museum, London, England

108: "Life Cycles of Two Moths," 1701–5, watercolor on vellum

Other Images

All photographs © Joyce Sidman 2018, except where otherwise noted

vi, viii, ix, 2–3, 7, 10, 14, 30, 35, 37, 45 (lower left), **61, 79, 100, 103, 113, 119**: Alamy.com

xii, xiii, 4, 5, 6, 9, 16-17, 53, 65, 67 (detail), **75, 87, 115** (detail), **124–29** (background map): Rijksmuseum, Amsterdam, Netherlands

8, 125 (detail): Frans Hals Museum, De Hallen Haarlem, Netherlands, Photo © Tom Haartsen

11, 13, 39, 88, 125 (detail): Gettyimages.com

18: Johann Andreas Graff, "Jacob Marrel's daughter Sara," 1658, Städel Museum, Frankfurt/Main, Germany, Photo © Städel Museum-ARTOTHEK

22, 24, 25: © Dwight Kuhn

32: HIP/Art Resource, NY

33: Johannes Goedart, "Frontispiece, Pars Secunda" (P.14,263) and "Plate 33" (P.14,270), hand-colored engravings, Minnich Collection, the Ethel Morrison Van Derlip Fund, 1966, Minneapolis Institute of Art, Minneapolis, Minnesota, Photos © Minneapolis Institute of Art

60: Staatsarchiv Nuremberg, Nuremberg, Germany

72: Photo ©Wiesbaden Museum, The Gerning Collection, Wiesbaden, Germany

117: Deutschmark image courtesy of Deutsche Bundesbank

INDEX

Page numbers appearing in **bold** denote illustration and photo captions.

★ "Combines lyrical poetry and compelling art with science concepts."
—*Booklist*, starred review

"A keenly perceptive poet, Sidman shows that both words and snow have the power to transform our view of things."
—*New York Times Book Review*

★ "An important book both for its creativity and for its wisdom."
—*School Library Journal*, starred review

★ "A work to be savored by young artists and scientists."
—*Kirkus Reviews*, starred review

★ "Will inspire a rainbow of uses."
—*The Bulletin*, starred review

★ "A celebratory story of survival."
—*Publishers Weekly*, starred review

★ "Poems of bravery, love, heartbreak, justice, and peace unite to offer readers of all ages solace, inspiration, and strength."
—*Publishers Weekly*, starred review